FYI *FOR STRATEGIC EFFECTIVENESS*™

ALIGNING PEOPLE

AND OPERATIONAL PRACTICES

TO STRATEGY

ROBERT W. EICHINGER
KIM E. RUYLE
DAVID O. ULRICH

TABLE OF CONTENTS

FYI FOR STRATEGIC EFFECTIVENESS™

DIMENSION VII: DEVELOPING FUTURE LEADERS

DIMENSION VIII: GOVERNANCE

FYI for Strategic Effectiveness™

WHY WE WROTE THIS BOOK

FYI for Strategic Effectiveness is a companion to the STRATEGIC EFFECTIVENESS ARCHITECT™, a toolkit designed to help organizations identify and align organizational capabilities and people practices in support of business strategy. Organizational capabilities embody the knowledge and skills of an organization; they're the things that a firm does well or perhaps not so well. They predict what customers are best served and what strategy is best pursued by an organization.

Organizational capabilities are typically described in behavioral terms. You can observe and measure them. You can set specific goals for them. You can teach them. Develop them. Or, you can ignore them.

Our toolkit, the STRATEGIC EFFECTIVENESS ARCHITECT™, is a comprehensive set of mission-critical organizational capabilities. Every successful firm will have a core set of these capabilities in which they are particularly skilled and which defines the organization.

You can use this book to facilitate action planning resulting from the use of the toolkit. Or, you can use it as a stand-alone guide to developing organizational capabilities.

A note about terminology: we've used the term "capability" when referring to organization-level skill sets. In general, we've used the term "competency" to refer to a skill possessed by individuals. Capabilities and competencies are related; capabilities can be mapped to competencies. And, in fact, an organizational capability only exists to the extent there are people with the particular combination of competencies that, taken together, result in a higher-level organizational strength, a capability. In practice, many people use the terms interchangeably, particularly when referring to "core competencies" to define a mission-critical set of organizational capabilities. Don't get too hung up on terminology. Just remember that organizations and people are alike in that both have strengths and weaknesses. The key is to know what you've got and what you need.

WHO IS THIS BOOK FOR?

Business leaders and senior management will find this book useful for strategic planning, developing core capabilities, auditing and enhancing corporate culture, and for facilitating mergers, acquisitions, and other major change initiatives.

I

WHAT IS THE STRATEGIC EFFECTIVENESS ARCHITECT™?

The STRATEGIC EFFECTIVENESS ARCHITECT™ is a toolkit, supported by a process that identifies the mix of people and organizational capabilities, cultural attributes, and leadership competencies that are mission-critical to the success of an enterprise. This toolkit and process is derived from the original work (ORGANIZATIONAL CULTRIBUTE ARCHITECT®) of Bob Eichinger and Mike Lombardo who, in collaboration with Dave Ulrich, defined the organizational capabilities that organizations must possess to successfully execute strategy.

A WORD ABOUT CULTRIBUTES

Originally, we coined the term "cultributes" to describe a combination of selected organizational capabilities, leadership competencies, and cultural attributes which may either support or oppose an organization's chances of implementing its strategy.

When cultributes are aligned with the business strategy, you can be more confident that you're aligning and integrating your people and organizational processes around the particular capabilities that are mission-critical to organizational success.

WHERE DID THE STRATEGIC EFFECTIVENESS ARCHITECT™ COME FROM?

The original 80 individual items in the CULTRIBUTES set were taken from research, relevant literature, case studies, and the combined experience of the authors in consulting with companies on strategy, management, and leadership.

The items were developed, tested, revised and statistically analyzed for relationship patterns that enabled the groupings under the 8 main dimensions around which this book has been developed.

To produce this updated and improved version, we looked at the continuing research since the introduction of the toolkit and surveyed users to see what needed changing and what needed to be added. Subsequently, based on new and emerging research and consulting experience, we expanded the set to 95 items, reexamined the clusters, and using the original research as a guide, published the revised toolkit as the STRATEGIC EFFECTIVENESS ARCHITECT™.

WHY LOOK AT THESE 95 ORGANIZATIONAL CAPABILITIES?

There are some universal principles that relate to organizational success:

Organizational form and function matter. Those organizations that align around customer needs are, of necessity, more flexible and adaptable, and therefore more competitive. They are, as well, more likely to create cultures that provide competitive advantage and are difficult for competitors to copy. If you're going to design your organization for success, then form should follow function. Identifying the key capabilities will address the organization's function.

Organizational agility matters. Competitors, labor markets, regulations, customer requirements, technology, economic conditions, and other factors are all changing more rapidly than ever before; all signs point to a continued rapid pace. If your organization doesn't have the flexibility and agility to adapt and change, you'll fall behind.

Organizations can be thought of as bundles of capabilities. Consider the example of two retail firms in a similar market space—one of which, Business X, prides itself on superior customer relationships, while the other, Business Y, touts its low prices. They've both decided to pursue a similar purpose: provide a broad array of name-brand home decorating accessories to a middle-class market. And they both have similar goals flowing from their strategies, including increasing their market share and growing globally. But the collection of particular capabilities each organization needs to support its overall strategy varies. These two organizations, similar in many respects, require people with different skills and motivations and will most benefit from different operational systems and cultures.

An organization's culture affects its ability to change. Since the business process reengineering movement of the late 1980s and on, one statistic stands out: approximately 66% of such initiatives have failed to achieve the goals that were set for them. The ratio of disappointments in mergers and acquisitions is similar. And the reasons are pretty clear—an organization's culture develops around its strategy and design, and as the organization succeeds, its culture tends to become stronger (and sometimes arrogant). But unless its leaders are also attending thoughtfully to the culture and keeping a close eye on the external environment, cultures will tend to become change-resistant rather than adaptive as they strengthen. If the environment doesn't change, the fact that the culture is change-resistant doesn't create a huge problem. But when something in the environment changes and new skills and attitudes and approaches are required, look out.

HOW DO THE 95 STRATEGIC EFFECTIVENESS ARCHITECT™ ITEMS RELATE TO MANAGER AND LEADER COMPETENCIES?

In many ways, these organizational capability items are like leader and manager competencies, except they are at an organizational rather than an individual level. For example, they are typically described in behavioral terms. Specific goals can be set for them. They can be observed and measured. They can be taught, developed, or ignored. And, of course, they require people with a particular set of competencies in order to be put into practice. Each of the 95 items, the 20 clusters, and the 8 dimensions are mapped back into the LEADERSHIP ARCHITECT® Competency Library. That is, for each item, we have mapped the individual competencies which leaders and managers need in order to be skilled in that organizational behavior. The mapping is in Appendix B to this book.

HOW IS THIS BOOK ORGANIZED?

Content is organized around the organizational capabilities that the STRATEGIC EFFECTIVENESS ARCHITECT™ defines and sorts into 8 main dimensions based on the analysis of data from many organizations that have used the toolkit. These dimensions are:

Dimension I: Strategic Accuracy and Clarity
Dimension II: Strategy Execution
Dimension III: Managing Innovation and Change
Dimension IV: Attracting/Retaining/Motivating Talent
Dimension V: Leveraging a Productive Culture
Dimension VI: Managing Profitability and Delivering Value
Dimension VII: Developing Future Leaders
Dimension VIII: Governance

To facilitate the analysis of these dimensions and the items within them, we have further grouped the capabilities into clusters (more narrowly defined thematic groupings). The resulting clusters are also more readily translated to competencies. There are 20 clusters (A–T) grouped within the dimensions as follows:

Dimension I: Strategic Accuracy and Clarity
Cluster A: Focusing on Core Organizational and Leadership Capabilities
Cluster B: Focusing on Customers
Cluster C: Having a Competitive Strategy

Dimension II: Strategy Execution
Cluster D: Aligning with Strategy
Cluster E: Execution and Decision Making

Dimension III: Managing Innovation and Change
Cluster F: Innovation Leadership
Cluster G: Organizational Learning

Dimension IV: Attracting/Retaining/Motivating Talent
Cluster H: Upgrading the Workforce
Cluster I: Engaging Employees
Cluster J: Accountability and Rewards

Dimension V: Leveraging a Productive Culture
Cluster K: Leveraging Culture
Cluster L: Managing Communication
Cluster M: Collaborating Across Boundaries
Cluster N: Managing Diversity

Dimension VI: Managing Profitability and Delivering Value
Cluster O: Basis for Competitive Advantage
Cluster P: Supply Chain Management (from Raw Material to Customer)
Cluster Q: Running a Profitable Business
Cluster R: Creating and Sustaining Value

Dimension VII: Developing Future Leaders
Cluster S: Filling the Talent Bench

Dimension VIII: Governance
Cluster T: Managing in the Best Way

The book chapters are at the cluster level and provide definitions, discussions, tips for development, and suggested readings at that level. Within the cluster chapters, however, you will find some tips addressed to the specific items within that cluster.

THE STRUCTURE OF THE BOOK

Each chapter addresses a cluster and includes the following sections:

- **Quotes** – To stimulate thinking about the particular cluster.
- **The Signpost** – A brief description of the cluster and its importance.
- **Items** – A list of the specific organizational capabilities contained in that particular cluster. Note that these items are numbered in the order they occur in the STRATEGIC EFFECTIVENESS ARCHITECT™; the numbers do not relate to anything other than to how they are sequenced in the toolkit.
- **Unskilled** – A list of descriptors that apply to organizations that do not demonstrate strength in that particular cluster.
- **Skilled** – A list of descriptors that apply to organizations that demonstrate exceptional strength in that particular cluster.
- **Some Causes** – A list of some of the root causes that can explain why your organization is weak in the cluster.
- **The Ten LEADERSHIP ARCHITECT® Competencies Most Associated with This Cluster (in order of connectedness)** – A listing of the ten most strongly related individual competencies from the LEADERSHIP ARCHITECT® that supports success in that cluster.
    - As indicated in the heading, the ordering of the ten competencies is based on the strength of the relationship between the competency and

V

the organizational capability—those higher in the list have a stronger relationship.

- Use the competency lists to understand what particular skills, experience, and knowledge leaders need to support that set of capabilities.

- Also, use these competencies in interviewing, selecting, assessing, developing, and deploying people.

- **The Map** – A description of the business landscape related to the cluster to help you and the people in your organization understand what the applicable organizational capabilities look like *in practice*.

- **Some Remedies** – Suggestions for actions to strengthen the organizational capabilities represented in the cluster.

  - These prescriptive recommendations are like items that you might find in an individual's development plan but are directed to the organizational level.

- **Suggested Readings** – A reference list of resources we've found useful in learning about and further exploring the themes in that cluster.

  - We've looked at both the theoretical and the practical, with a bias toward practical, accessible references that will serve as springboards to your understanding of best practices and applications.

Each cluster stands on its own with the information provided to answer the basic question: What does it take to do this as well as it can be done?

WHAT CAN THE STRATEGIC EFFECTIVENESS ARCHITECT™ DO FOR YOUR ORGANIZATION?

There are many ways to use the toolkit to drive success in your organization:

1. **Create an operational system that is aligned with strategy.** The toolkit will help you define and communicate your best competitive strategy. When everyone in the organization shares a language and common mind-set, you'll be better able to create processes that minimize friction and increase the efficiency of decision making, resource allocation, and initiatives. Alignment is the key. Everything needs to align with your strategy—policies, rewards, processes, organizational structure, and the deployment of your talent. Alignment leads to excellence in execution.

2. **Align your strategy with organizational capabilities.** Use the toolkit to take inventory of your capabilities, to identify your organization's strengths and weaknesses. When your organizational capabilities are present in the right combination and at the right level, they will fuel your success. They're the skills that will drive your business strategy and help you achieve operational excellence.

3. **Create a success profile for leaders and managers.** After using the toolkit to identify core organizational capabilities, you'll want to map them to the individual competencies your leaders and managers need. These competencies will guide the selection, development, promotion, and retention of talent aligned with your business strategy. For confirmation of those competencies, you can access a number of research- and experience-based job profiles (competency models) in Lominger's SUCCESS PROFILE ARCHITECT® (SPA) toolkit. These profiles include the top 22 competencies for various positions by role, job level, job function, and more. While most successful organizations have a pretty good idea about the types of jobs required to get the work done, the organizations that go the extra step to ensure an optimal alignment between jobs and the requirements of the business strategy gain a significant competitive advantage.

4. **Assess your culture.** Culture is typically thought of as the way things get done, the sum of the collective habits of the individuals in the organization. In large measure, your core capabilities are observable in organizational and individual behavior. The 95 items explained in the toolkit, when aligned with individual, managerial, and leadership competencies, point the way to the essential behavioral and knowledge components of work—combinations of skills, behaviors, and knowledge that are largely learned from experience in the context of your culture. Culture is a key component of success.

5. **Assess the feasibility of M&A.** Use the toolkit to both assess organizations and to do a gap analysis. The results will identify the challenges and degree of difficulty you will face in melding the organizations. The outcome will point to an effective action plan for managing change and merging the capabilities and cultures to achieve a realistic blend that is aligned with your post–M&A business strategy.

Any organization can gain competitive advantage by using the STRATEGIC EFFECTIVENESS ARCHITECT™ toolkit. But there are some specific things that indicate your organization will clearly benefit. If your organization…

- Has a stated vision and values but isn't getting traction with them
- Wants to understand what drives the type of culture you have
- Wants to link competencies to strategy and the business proposition
- Knows it needs to change the culture but doesn't know how or where to start
- Has stalled, reached a plateau, and/or become inflexible
- Is spending lots of money on various initiatives and is not seeing results
- Is doing a lot of different things without focus
- Has scattered pockets of success but overall inconsistency
- Has lots of HR interventions going on but little senior leader involvement or championing

- Is planning to go through, or has recently gone through, a merger or acquisition
- Is planning business process reengineering and/or restructuring
- Is struggling to align the organizational strategy to leadership competencies and HR systems
- Is as interested in what it *could be* in relation to what it currently is or is not

…then you are ripe for the use of the STRATEGIC EFFECTIVENESS ARCHITECT™, and this book is for you.

With the tips and resources this book provides, those who are responsible for organizational change, culture management, and business process alignment will find it easier to create the kind of goal-based action plans that are essential in making your strategy work. While the book is intended to support users of the STRATEGIC EFFECTIVENESS ARCHITECT™ toolkit, it can also stand alone as a guide to developing the critical capabilities of organizations.

And that's what this book is about. It's about strategy. About organizational capabilities. About talent management practices. Our message is that organizational effectiveness is driven through the alignment of these three—business strategy, organizational capabilities, and talent management practices.

Effective organizations select a differentiating strategy based on self-awareness and deep knowledge of customers, competitors, and the business landscape. They select a winning strategy and they execute it. They have people who are capable of execution. Talented people. Skilled people. Motivated, engaged people. All this spells success!

Robert W. Eichinger

Kim E. Ruyle

Dave O. Ulrich

ABOUT THE AUTHORS

BOB EICHINGER

Bob Eichinger is CEO of Lominger International, A Korn/Ferry Company and cofounder of Lominger Limited. He is cocreator of The LEADERSHIP ARCHITECT® Suite of management, executive, and organizational development tools. During his 40+ year career, he has worked inside PepsiCo and Pillsbury, and as a consultant in Fortune 500 companies in the U.S., Europe, Japan, Canada, and Australia. Bob lectures extensively on the topic of executive and management development and has served on the Board of the Human Resource Planning Society. He has worked as a coach with more than 1,000 managers and executives. Bob's books include *The Leadership Machine*, written with Mike Lombardo, and *100 Things You Need to Know: Best People Practices for Managers & HR,* written with Mike Lombardo and Dave Ulrich.

KIM RUYLE

Kim Ruyle is vice president of product for Lominger International. He started his career in the skilled trades, taught at several universities, founded and managed a software company, and held management positions in Fortune 500 and Global 100 organizations. In the human resource and learning and development fields, Kim has presented at national and international conferences, authored over a dozen book chapters and articles, and served on numerous expert panels.

DAVE ULRICH

Dave Ulrich has been listed by *BusinessWeek* as the top "guru" in management education. He has coauthored more than a dozen books and over 100 articles, serves on the Board of Directors of Herman Miller, and has consulted with over half of the Fortune 200. Dave is a professor at the Ross School of Business at the University of Michigan.

ACKNOWLEDGEMENTS

We are indebted to a number of people who contributed ideas and assistance in the preparation of this book.

Mike Lombardo was a key researcher and codeveloper of the original CULTRIBUTES® product on which the STRATEGIC EFFECTIVENESS ARCHITECT™ was based. We are deeply indebted to his substantial contribution to the body of knowledge around organizational effectiveness and alignment.

John Kulas, Linda Rodman, Michael Harper, and Michelle Weitzman shared their expertise and contributed key content.

Ken De Meuse, George Hallenbeck, Lisa-Marie Hanson, Paul Stiles, and Guangrong Dai, all from the outstanding product research and development team at Lominger International, reviewed our work and made many helpful suggestions.

Diane Hoffmann, Lesley Kurke, and Eric Ekstrand, also on the product team at Lominger International, did a phenomenal job of pushing the book through to production.

Bonnie Parks did her customary excellent job of proofreading and editing our manuscript.

We appreciate the contribution of all.

CLUSTER A: FOCUSING ON CORE ORGANIZATIONAL AND LEADERSHIP CAPABILITIES

Sometimes, we just don't know enough about what we are trying to achieve.
Stuart Wilde – Author and lecturer

*I've seen a great many people who are exceedingly good at execution,
but exceedingly poor at picking the important things.*
Peter Drucker – Business theorist, author, and strategist

THE SIGNPOST

To begin, get in the right mind-set. Design your business strategy to leverage your core organizational capabilities. Play to your strengths. When you do, you'll remove friction and noise from your operations. Your teams will be more engaged and motivated to execute tactical plans. In short, you'll be more successful.

ITEMS

1. Clearly understand the business(es) we are in and want to be in
21. Know what our core technical/functional capabilities and unique strengths are
41. Understand what our core leadership capabilities and unique strengths are
61. Understand what our core organizational capabilities and unique strengths are
79. Have a business strategy built around and aligned with our core organizational capabilities
90. Build or acquire the core business or organizational capabilities that are required, given our strategic outlook, and discard outmoded ones

UNSKILLED

- Does not understand the organization's strengths and weaknesses
- Is not totally clear about the mission and purpose of the business
- Doesn't fully understand the business landscape, the market, the competition
- Can't shape or build new and needed capabilities
- Fails to develop strategy that is matched with core capabilities
- Does not or cannot think about the organization in terms of capabilities
- Hangs on to old and outmoded capabilities too long

SKILLED

- Develops a clear sense of purpose for the organization aligned with customer needs
- Clearly articulates the organization's core capabilities

1

- Identifies and defines the key products and services that flow from core capabilities
- Matches up core capabilities with various strategic choices
- Designs an effective process to build or acquire missing core capabilities
- Describes the relationship between core capabilities and customer needs
- Quickly pinpoints market opportunities that can be leveraged by core capabilities

SOME CAUSES

- Lack of understanding about how organizations work
- Mistaken assumptions about what customers need and want
- Inability to accurately size up people
- Organization not viewed as a whole
- Incomplete connection between capabilities, customers, and strategy
- Unclear view of the future
- Reliance on past accomplishments

THE TEN LEADERSHIP ARCHITECT® COMPETENCIES MOST ASSOCIATED WITH THIS CLUSTER (in order of connectedness)

5. Business Acumen

46. Perspective

58. Strategic Agility

2. Dealing with Ambiguity

17. Decision Quality

51. Problem Solving

56. Sizing Up People

50. Priority Setting

52. Process Management

65. Managing Vision and Purpose

THE MAP

Individuals have strengths and weaknesses. So do organizations. Teams, business units, entire enterprises have particular skills and competencies. An organization might be characterized as being slow or fast. Creative or stale. Innovative or dull. Proactive or reactive. Risk taking or risk averse. These and other attributes in combination with the inventory of organizational capabilities give each firm a distinctive complexion—a profile shaped by a combination of history, the current context, and the collective skills and weaknesses of the people in the organization. Organization capabilities can have an enabling or chilling effect. When they're present in the right combination and at the right level, they fuel an organization's business activities and success. When they're insufficient (or missing entirely), they become an anchor that holds the organization back. An organization that is too deliberate and overly reflective

2

will struggle in a fast-paced market. To a great extent, the current inventory of organizational capabilities dictates which strategies a company can successfully pursue. If the desired business strategy requires capabilities that are not in the organization's current inventory, there are two options: (a) change the strategy or (b) acquire/build the competencies. Be crystal clear about your core capabilities. Generally, they will fall in one of three buckets. Technical/functional capabilities are specific to an industry or market. Examples include specialized skills required to process rare metals and engineering expertise related to fiber optics. A second category of core capabilities, organizational capabilities, are targeted business skills. Examples include the ability to very rapidly analyze changes in market demands and expertise in supply chain management. Finally, there are general leadership capabilities. These are things like comfort with uncertainty, change management skills, and strategic agility. These three buckets of skills add up to what we refer to as the core capabilities of the enterprise. They're the skills that drive business strategy and operational excellence. The particular combination of core capabilities possessed by any organization will predict what it can do most successfully in the marketplace.

SOME REMEDIES

1. **Get educated.** If your organization doesn't think about the organization in terms of its core capabilities, get started. Have everyone in top management read three books or articles on the subject (see reading list below). Have them report on what they have read. Collect the lessons. Share the lessons. Talk about them. Produce a report on how all of this applies to your organization. Bring in a top core-competency consultant to further educate top management and establish a foundation on which to build capabilities in the organization.

2. **Audit your capabilities.** Do a core capability survey. There are a number of commercially available surveys you can use. Have top management and one level below complete the survey. Produce a report and have a core capability off-site workshop to discuss the results. You should end up with a map that details your capability inventory and the gaps between what you have and what you need. Guard against developing arrogance around what you're best at. You've got gaps to fill.

3. **Plan.** Connect the dots. On the wall in your conference room, you need three boards. On the first, describe what your customers want, what they need, and what they expect from you and your competitors. On the second board, describe your strategic objectives—the key elements of your winning business plan. The third board is for your core capabilities. List them in the three categories of core capabilities: technical/functional, organizational, and leadership. Now, connect the dots. Where are the gaps? Can you pull the story together? Does it make sense?

3

4. **Hire expertise.** Hire a person into your strategic management function who has successfully done core competency work in other companies. But don't just delegate the competency work and think the job is done. You need a leader for the effort, but the leader won't do it all. Your key leaders must be engaged in the process.

5. **Study competitors.** Do an analysis of all of your competitors. What are they good at? What are their weaknesses? How do you compare? Speed? Customer service? New products and services? Global reach? Talent management? Etc.

6. **Assess managers.** Senior managers should be fluent in describing the core capabilities of their units and explaining how these capabilities are developed. Have them adopt this as a formal goal and appraise them on it. Do they get it? Do they communicate it? Do they develop their unit's core capabilities?

7. **Assess people.** Create an assessment program for the top three levels in your organization. Use the core competencies you have identified as critical for success and assess each person against those competencies. Have management work with individuals to create personalized development plans to fill gaps.

8. **Build competencies.** Fill the gaps between your existing and desired competencies with training and development. Be realistic about what can be accomplished with training courses. They will be most effective in building the technical/functional competencies, somewhat less so in strengthening organizational competencies, and much less so in enhancing leadership competencies. All sound training will consist of content, practice, and assessment. You need all three. The transfer of training back to the job is most critical—you need to ensure that what's learned in training is retained and applied on the job. Managers and supervisors must be involved in the transfer of training to make sure that people have opportunities to apply what they've learned and receive feedback on their performance. Most of your competency gaps can only be partially addressed by training. People learn most of what they know by doing on the job and by working with others. Look to development activities such as special assignments to complete the picture.

9. **Acquire competencies.** Fill the gaps between your existing and desired competencies with a combination of hiring, acquiring, or partnering. This might be a quick way to close competency gaps and effective in the short-term. For a long-term competitive advantage, you need to internalize the ability to build competencies that are in short supply and not easily replicated by your competitors. Then, you need to retain and continue to develop your talent.

10. **Engage your board.** Get your directors involved in defining organizational capabilities and addressing gaps. Most boards have directors with significant business experience. They've run businesses in the past or maybe do so currently. They will have a good idea about your organization's core capabilities. Ask them.

SUGGESTED READINGS

Campbell, A., & Sommers Luchs, K. (1997). *Core competency based strategy.* Stamford, CT: International Thomson Business Press.

Drejer, A. (2002). *Strategic management and core competencies: Theory and application.* Westport, CT: Quorum Books.

Hamel, G., & Heene, A. (1994). *Competence based competition.* Chichester, UK: John Wiley & Sons.

Hamel, G., & Prahalad, C. K. (1990 May/June). The core competence of the corporation. *Harvard Business Review, 68*(3), 79-93.

Hamel, G., & Prahalad, C. K. (1994). *Competing for future.* Boston, MA: Harvard Business School Press.

Kim, W. C., & Mauborgne, R. (2005). *Blue ocean strategy: How to create uncontested market space and make competition irrelevant.* Boston, MA: Harvard Business School Press.

Mascarenhas, B., Baveja, A., & Jamil, M. (1998). Dynamics of core competencies in leading multinational companies. *California Management Review, 40*(4), 117-132.

Porter, M. E. (1998a). *Competitive advantage: Creating and sustaining superior performance.* New York: Free Press.

Porter, M. E. (1998b). *Competitive strategy: Techniques for analyzing industries and competitors.* New York, NY: Free Press.

Schoemaker, P. J. H. (1992). How to link strategic vision to core capabilities. *Sloan Management Review, 34*(1). 67-81.

Zook, C. (2004). *Beyond the core: Expand your market without abandoning your roots.* Boston, MA: Harvard Business School Press.

Zook, C., & Allen, J. (2001). *Profit from the core: Growth strategy in an era of turbulence.* Boston, MA: Harvard Business School Press.

CLUSTER B: FOCUSING ON CUSTOMERS

Your most unhappy customers are your greatest source of learning.
Bill Gates – Co-founder, Microsoft

*Customer satisfaction is achieved when you sell merchandise
that doesn't come back to a customer that does.*
H. Stanley Marcus – Former Chairman, Neiman-Marcus

THE SIGNPOST

Look to your customers. Never take them for granted. Without them, you don't have a business. Make customers the centerpiece of your strategy. Every business equation should include a customer factor that reflects the impact of decisions on customers. There are many ways to organize a business, many options for developing products and services, and lots of ways in which to deliver those products and services. Make every decision with your customers in mind. They'll reward you with their business.

ITEMS

2. Know who our most profitable customers are
22. Customize and tailor our products and services to fit key customers
42. Understand our customers and their needs
62. Maintain strong key customer connectedness and relationships
80. Have a process for gathering and acting on customer feedback and suggestions

UNSKILLED

- Ignores the voice of the customer
- Misunderstands how customers perceive the organization
- Does not include customer feedback in product and service decisions
- Doesn't deliver what the customer really wants
- Makes customers feel undervalued
- Does not differentiate among customers; doesn't segment customers
- Is not organized around the customer

SKILLED

- Consistently solicits, compiles, and analyzes customer input
- Understands and listens to the voice of the customer
- Considers customers' needs and requirements in product and service offerings
- Is intimately familiar with the business operations or personal habits of customers

- Has extensive knowledge about competitive products and services
- Balances the needs of the business and the needs of the customer in decision making
- Organizes business processes to best serve customer needs

SOME CAUSES

- Organizational arrogance
- Failure to listen
- Comfort with the status quo
- Slow to change and act
- Unorganized
- Narrow perspective
- Slow to make decisions
- Organizational defensiveness

THE TEN LEADERSHIP ARCHITECT® COMPETENCIES MOST ASSOCIATED WITH THIS CLUSTER (in order of connectedness)

15. Customer Focus

33. Listening

51. Problem Solving

56. Sizing Up People

52. Process Management

64. Understanding Others

5. Business Acumen

12. Conflict Management

46. Perspective

53. Drive for Results

THE MAP

Business starts and ends with a customer. Great products, talented employees, outstanding processes—they're all for naught without a customer. A winning business strategy is designed around the customer. It places the customer squarely in the middle. Execution of the strategy will ensure that you're meeting and exceeding your customer expectations. Over time, the organizations that consistently win are the ones that most accurately anticipate customer needs and deliberately design business processes to deliver on those needs. The best organizations don't wait for the customer to come to them. They go to the customer. They become intimately knowledgeable of customer needs, the ways in which customers use their products, the way customers talk about their products. Organizations ask questions. Lots of questions. They watch. They learn. Then they innovate, improve, respond. They never get defensive. Organizations

8

develop an intimacy with their customers so they understand not only how customers use their products, but how they prefer to buy products, how they value the products, how and when they dispose of the products. This is a never-ending cycle of customer focus that keeps successful organizations relevant and growing.

SOME REMEDIES

1. **Segment your customers.** For most businesses, the 80/20 rule applies. Twenty percent of your customers are returning 80% of your results. Consider a CRM (customer relationship management) system, if you don't already have one, to help you manage your customer relationships. Rank your customers on revenue and their contribution to the bottom line. Align your organization to pay closest attention to the top 20% and decreasing attention to those further down the list. There are some customers that may be more trouble than they're worth. Figure out how to change the relationship and value proposition. If you can't, "fire" them.

2. **Talk to your customers.** Formalize the dialog with customers. Make sure you are listening, especially to your top 20%. Have a well-defined process to collect and summarize customer feedback on a continuous basis. Know the trends. Figure out what's next. Be proactive to meet the future customer expectations.

3. **Audit your effectiveness.** Get the voice of the customer. Survey your customers on a continuous basis. If necessary, hire an outside survey firm to sample your customers. What do they like about your products and services? What don't they like? Measure customer satisfaction, loyalty/retention, and expansion as part of your balanced scorecard for business performance.

4. **Perform loss analysis.** Track lost customers. Why did they stop using your products and services? What could have saved them? Can you bring them back? How can you prevent that kind of loss from happening again? Figure out ways to make it easier for your customers to do business with you.

5. **Hold people accountable.** Every employee should consider how they can include meaningful customer-related goals in their individual performance goals. Develop customer-service skills in all business functions. Build rewards and recognition for superior customer focus into your performance management and talent management systems.

6. **Know your competitors.** Conduct an analysis to contrast competitive products and services with yours. What are their strengths? Weaknesses? Why do customers go to your competitors? What does the competition provide that you don't? What more can you do? How can you leapfrog the competition?

7. **Stay connected.** Focus on building productive relationships. Do you have a key account organization? Who is accountable for key customers? Who owns them?

What about top management? Do they get out into the field to meet customers? Do they have personal relationships with key customers? How often are key customers invited in to visit? What have you done to recognize their value, to make them feel as special as they really are to your organization?

8. **Involve customers.** Invite key customers in to help create new products and services or to improve existing offerings. Create a process for formally collecting and analyzing customer ideas. Many customers love to be asked. When you get ideas, follow through. Show your appreciation. Keep them posted on the application of their ideas.

9. **Get customer-centric.** Are you organized to serve your customers? How are responses to customer requests handled? How fast can decisions be made? Are the resources aligned with delivering the response? How are complaints handled? Are they summarized for trends? Organize to address these issues. Apply business process engineering to improve handoffs and customer touch points.

10. **Tailor your offerings.** Do you have the processes and capacity to customize and tailor your products and services to individual key customers? How many options are you providing in product features? Service? Upgrades? Applications? Purchase? Financing? Delivery? Flexibility in product offerings and distribution channels has become the norm.

SUGGESTED READINGS

Ang, L., & Buttle, F. (2006). Customer retention management processes: A quantitative study. *European Journal of Marketing, 40*, 83-99.

Duffy, D. L. (2005). The evolution of customer loyalty strategy. *Journal of Consumer Marketing, 22*, 284-286.

Freeland, J. (2002). *The ultimate CRM handbook: Strategies and concepts for building enduring customer loyalty and profitability.* New York, NY: McGraw-Hill.

Gitomer, J. (1998). *Customer satisfaction is worthless, customer loyalty is priceless: How to make customers love you, keeping them coming back and tell everyone they know.* Austin, TX: Bard Press.

Griffin, J. (2002). *Customer loyalty: How to earn it, how to keep it* (new and revised edition). San Francisco, CA: Jossey-Bass.

Johnson, M. D., Gustafsson, A. (2001). *Improving customer satisfaction, loyalty, and profit: An integrated measurement and management system.* San Francisco, CA: Jossey-Bass Inc.

Johnson, M. D., Hermann, A., & Huber, F. (2006). The evolution of loyalty intentions. *Journal of Marketing, 70*, 122-132.

McConnell, B., & Huba, J. (2002). *Creating customer evangelists: How loyal customers become a volunteer sales force.* Chicago, IL: Dearborn Trade Publishing.

Peppers, D., & Rogers, M. (2004). *Managing customer relationships: A strategic framework.* Hoboken, NJ: John Wiley & Sons.

Porter, M. E. (1998). *Competitive strategy: Techniques for analyzing industries and competitors.* New York, NY: Free Press.

Prahalad, C. K., & Ramaswamy, V. (2004). *The future of competition: Co-creating unique value with customers.* Boston, MA: Harvard Business School Press.

Reichheld, F. F., & Teal, T. (2001). *The loyalty effect: The hidden force behind growth, profits, and lasting value.* Boston, MA: Harvard Business School Press.

Rowley, J. (2005). The four Cs of customer loyalty. *Marketing Intelligence & Planning, 23*, 574-581.

Sewell, C., & Brown, P. B. (2002). *Customers for life: How to turn that one-time buyer into a lifetime customer.* New York, NY: Doubleday.

Thompson, H. (2004). *Who stole my customer? Winning strategies for creating the sustaining customer loyalty.* Upper Saddle River, NJ: Pearson Education, Inc.

Treacy, M., & Wiersema, F. (1993, January/February). Customer intimacy and other value disciplines. *Harvard Business Review, 71*(1), 84-93.

Treacy, M., & Wiersema, F. (1997). *The discipline of market leaders: Choose your customers, narrow your focus, dominate your market*. New York, NY: Perseus Books Group.

Ulwick, A. (2005). *What customers want: Using outcome-driven innovation to create breakthrough products and services*. New York, NY: McGraw-Hill.

Wayland, R. E., & Cole, P. M. (1997). *Customer connections: New strategies for growth*. Boston, MA: Harvard Business School Press.

Wiersema, F. (2002). *The new market leaders: Who's winning and how in the battle for customers*. New York, NY: Free Press.

CLUSTER C: HAVING A COMPETITIVE STRATEGY

*The general who wins the battle makes many calculations
in his temple before the battle is fought. The general who loses
makes but few calculations beforehand.*
Sun Tzu – Military strategist and author (6th century B.C.)

However beautiful the strategy, you should occasionally look at the results.
Sir Winston Churchill – British Prime Minister
and winner of the Nobel Prize in Literature

THE SIGNPOST

Create a competitive strategy, a high-level plan to apply energy and resources over your long-term planning horizon. An effective strategy will uniquely serve your customers, leverage your organizational capabilities, differentiate you from the competition, and be difficult for others to replicate. Your strategic plan will define what your business is going to look like and how it's going to create value for its stakeholders. Without a sound competitive strategy, you'll wander in the wilderness and be eaten by the competition. With the right competitive strategy, you'll dominate your market.

ITEMS

3. Have a clear point of view about the future of our industry and how we position ourselves in it to win
23. Assess competitor strategies and capabilities
43. Have a viable and successful annual business planning process
63. Make competitive product and marketplace decisions
81. Have a strategy in place to grow sustainable revenue and profitability over the long-term

UNSKILLED

- Finds it difficult to envision the future
- Is risk averse; too timid in the marketplace
- Fails to effectively gather competitive intelligence
- Plans ineffectively; creates plans that aren't realistic and actionable
- Is not creative or innovative
- Is sluggish, slow to act
- Waffles on decisions; is not decisive
- Trades long-term sustainability for near-term results

SKILLED

- Creates a clear vision of the future and thinks through multiple success scenarios
- Is clear about organizational capabilities
- Thoroughly understands the strengths and weaknesses of competitors
- Develops a set of robust strategies to pursue
- Clearly translates the strategy into an actionable plan
- Makes sound product and marketplace decisions quickly
- Faces reality when analyzing strengths and weaknesses
- Intuitively recognizes business opportunities before others

SOME CAUSES

- Not forward thinking; focused too much on the present or past
- Impatience with planning
- Crisis mentality
- Not market savvy
- Narrow perspective
- Inability to focus
- Unable to face reality

THE TEN LEADERSHIP ARCHITECT® COMPETENCIES MOST ASSOCIATED WITH THIS CLUSTER (in order of connectedness)

5. Business Acumen
46. Perspective
51. Problem Solving
15. Customer Focus
58. Strategic Agility
2. Dealing with Ambiguity
50. Priority Setting
17. Decision Quality
28. Innovation Management
52. Process Management

THE MAP

Where are you going? How will you get there? Executives and senior managers are often better at execution than strategy. Typical executives and managers are good at taking hills but not as good at picking the best hills to take. They do things in the right way. But they don't always do the right things. It takes both strategy and execution. Strategy is about the right things. Strategy starts by asking questions about the customer. Who is the target customer? Get specific. Define the customer segment clearly. Now ask what it is that customers want and need. For what are they willing to pay?

Again, get specific. Consider the external environment. Where are the opportunities? Where are the threats? Where is the competition entrenched? Strong? Weak? Create a detailed picture of the business landscape that includes your target customers, the competition, and all the other external factors that impact the scene—regulatory issues, environmental issues, socioeconomic issues, etc. Paint multiple versions of the picture—the current landscape and the future landscape. Until the picture is clear, you can't develop an effective strategy. Once you've defined the external world, you can turn the focus inward. You'll land on a successful strategy when you've considered your inventory of core capabilities—the skills at which the organization excels. The winning ticket is to select a strategy based on what the customer needs, opportunities revealed in the business landscape, and alignment with your core capabilities. Accurate and clear strategy guides decision making, resource allocation, and staffing. It increases speed. It helps define best practices from an operational point of view and minimizes mistakes, backing up and having to try again. Winning, then, is a combination of three things: (1) a distinct and accurate strategy centered on the customer and considering the business landscape, (2) a clear and unbiased understanding of what the organization can do, and (3) knowledge of how to fill the gap.

SOME REMEDIES

1. **Get strategic.** Devote time to thinking about strategy. Step back. See the big picture. Look to the future. Three years. Five years. Ten years. Create a shared vision. What will be different? The same? Be specific. If your organization lacks strategic perspective, start by having everyone in top management read three books or articles on strategy (see reading list below). Have each member of management report on what they have read. Take the time to discuss it, to contrast learnings, perspectives, and views of the future. Get people together. Get them talking. Thinking. Focusing on success. On the future. On your strategy.

2. **Get help.** You don't have to do it all yourself. Consider retaining a top strategy consultant to help get top management educated and to craft a winning strategy. Consider hiring someone into your strategic management function who has successfully led strategic planning in other companies. Have that person lead the effort, craft communications about the strategy, facilitate planning sessions, and help get leadership engaged.

3. **Use consistent strategic language.** Define the vocabulary that describes your strategy and your core capabilities. Talk the talk. Reinforce the message and vocabulary at every opportunity. We think with words. A common language is critical to arriving at a shared understanding in the organization. Be consistent in using that language.

4. **Study competitors.** Do an analysis of all of your competitors. Study their annual reports. Study every article, every press release, everything written about your competition. What is their strategy as it relates to speed, customer service, new products and services, global reach and talent? How do their strategies compare to yours? What's the same? What's different? What is your competitive edge? Determine where you have competitive blind spots.

5. **Engage managers.** Involve managers at all levels in strategic planning for their own unit and at least one level above. Add strategy formulation and strategic skills to their individual development plan and appraise them on those skills. Identify those that are particularly skilled in strategic agility, perspective, dealing with ambiguity, and managing vision and purpose. Engage them as mentors for managers who are not as skilled.

6. **Assess people.** Create an assessment program for the top three levels in your organization. Use the core capabilities you have identified as critical to your success and assess each person against those capabilities. Follow up with individualized development plans to close gaps and build the competencies needed for success.

7. **Build strategic competencies.** Design development opportunities to strengthen skills in strategy. Assign managers and key employees to organizational committees, task forces, and special projects for development. Employ action learning to get managers involved in solving real business problems while they collaborate and learn. Senior managers and board members should mentor, coach, and evaluate solutions created by project teams. Look for extracurricular learning activities that teach and reinforce strategic thinking, things such as serving on the board of a nonprofit or professional organization. Team up with a local university to create a strategy course or curriculum.

8. **Acquire strategic capabilities.** Those capabilities that can't be built fast enough can be filled by a combination of hiring, acquiring, or partnering. Create a strategic staffing plan to hire what you have trouble developing. Look at the possibility of acquisitions or strategic alliances that will fill gaps in core capabilities. Do what it takes.

9. **Engage your board.** If you're not using your board to contribute to strategy, what are you using them for? Most boards have directors who currently or in the past have run a business. Tap into their strategic expertise. Use them to actively partner with senior management to craft business strategy.

10. **Dive into the future.** Read voraciously—history, business journals, biographies, and the work of futurists. Use everything you read to challenge your thoughts about the future. Get in the habit of questioning. When you encounter a new idea, learn of a new societal trend, read about a new business model—when you

learn about anything new and interesting—ask yourself what it will mean for the future. Consider hiring a futurist to consult with your top management team to develop scenarios that most likely will impact your organization in the future.

SUGGESTED READINGS

Aaker, D. A. (2001). *Developing business strategies* (6th ed.). New York, NY: John Wiley & Sons, Inc.

Brown, S., & Eisenhardt, K. (1998). *Competing on the edge*. Boston, MA: Harvard Business School Press.

Christensen, C. M., Roth, E. A., & Anthony, S. D. (2004). *Seeing what's next: Using theories of innovation to predict industry change*. Boston, MA: Harvard Business School Press.

Dussauge, P., & Garrette, B. (1999). *Corporative strategy: Competing successfully through strategic alliances*. New York, NY: John Wiley & Sons, Inc.

Gottfredson, M., & Aspinall, K. (2005, November). Innovation vs. complexity. *Harvard Business Review, 83*(11), 62-71.

Hamel, G., & Prahalad, C. K. (1996). *Competing for the future*. Boston, MA: Harvard Business School Press.

Hussey, D., & Jenster, P. (1999). *Competitor intelligence*. New York, NY: John Wiley & Sons, Inc.

Kaufman, J. J. (1998). *Value management: Creating competitive advantage*. Mississauga, ON: Crisp Learning.

Kim, W. C., & Mauborgne, R. (2005). *Blue ocean strategy: How to create uncontested market space and make competition irrelevant*. Boston, MA: Harvard Business School Press.

Mintzberg, H. (1994). *The rise and fall of strategic planning*. New York, NY: Free Press.

Moore, G. A. (2005, December). Strategy and your stronger hand. *Harvard Business Review, 83*(12), 62-72.

Oster, S. (1999). *Modern competitive analysis*. New York, NY: Oxford University Press.

Pearce, J. A., & Robinson, R. B. (2004). *Foundation, implementation, and control of competitive strategy* (9th ed.). New York, NY: McGraw-Hill.

Porter, M. E. (1996, November/December). What is strategy? *Harvard Business Review, 74*(6), 61-78.

Porter, M. E. (1998a). *Competitive advantage: Creating and sustaining superior performance*. New York, NY: Free Press.

Porter, M. E. (1998b). *Competitive strategy: Techniques for analyzing industries and competitors*. New York: Free Press.

Smith, J. L., & Flanagan, W. G. (2006). *Creating competitive advantage: Give customers a reason to choose you over your competitors*. New York: Currency.

Stalk, G., Jr. (1988, July/August). Time—The next source of competitive advantage. *Harvard Business Review, 66*(4), 41-51.

Sun Tzu (app. 500 B.C.). *The art of war* (L. Giles Trans., 2005). El Paso, Texas: El Paso Norte Press.

Toffler, A. (1980). *The third wave*. New York, NY: Bantam Books.

Treacy, M., & Wiersema, F. (1997). *The discipline of market leaders: Choose your customers, narrow your focus, dominate your market*. New York, NY: Perseus Books Group.

Trout, J., & Rivkin, S. (2000). *Differentiate or die: Survival in our era of killer competition*. New York, NY: John Wiley & Sons, Inc.

Ulwick, A. (2005). *What customers want: Using outcome-driven innovation to create breakthrough products and services*. New York: McGraw-Hill.

Whiteley, R., & Hessan, D. (1996). *Customer-centered growth: Five proven strategies for building competitive advantage*. New York: The Forum Corporation.

CLUSTER D: ALIGNING WITH STRATEGY

*Set your expectations high; find men and women whose integrity
and values you respect; get their agreement on a course of action;
and give them your ultimate trust.*
John Akers – Former Chairman, IBM

*Coming together is a beginning. Keeping together is progress.
Working together is success.*
Henry Ford – Founder, Ford Motor Company

THE SIGNPOST

It's not enough to create a great competitive strategy. You need alignment. Everyone needs to be aligned. People must understand and share a common view of the future. They must share commitment to the strategic goals. Everything needs to be aligned. Processes, goals, rewards, communication, policies—everything aligned. A small team pulling in the same direction will beat a larger team working at cross-purposes every time.

ITEMS

4. Continually shape the organization's structure and work flows to meet the changes and challenges of our marketplace
24. Apply total work systems (e.g., TQM/ISO/Six Sigma) where needed
44. Efficiently and effectively communicate our strategy to all employees
64. Align people policies, practices, and programs to support our business strategy
82. Identify the management and leadership competencies that our strategy requires

UNSKILLED

- Can't craft a compelling vision
- Communicates poorly
- Fails to set appropriate goals
- Doesn't reward the right things
- Is unable to design effective processes
- Is unwilling or unable to change, to adapt
- Lacks clarity in adopting policies and procedures
- Does not hold people accountable

SKILLED

- Communicates a clear, compelling vision
- Sincerely believes in and is passionate about the strategy
- Provides timely and relevant information to all who need it
- Sets aggressive goals that cascade down through the organization
- Has a process orientation; can effectively engineer business processes
- Has an eye for talent and selects the very best people for the role
- Possesses clarity of purpose and focuses resources and energy appropriately
- Drives the message about competitive strategy to every corner of the organization
- Rewards the behaviors that support the strategy

SOME CAUSES

- Fuzzy strategic vision
- Dysfunctional culture
- Lack of process discipline
- Mixed messages
- Poor listening
- Actions don't match message
- Lacking perspective
- Inattentive to details, can't execute
- Conflict avoidance
- Rigid, unwilling or unable to adapt

THE TEN LEADERSHIP ARCHITECT® COMPETENCIES MOST ASSOCIATED WITH THIS CLUSTER (in order of connectedness)

51. Problem Solving
52. Process Management
50. Priority Setting
2. Dealing with Ambiguity
47. Planning
58. Strategic Agility
5. Business Acumen
46. Perspective
63. Total Work Systems (e.g., TQM/ISO/Six Sigma)
65. Managing Vision and Purpose

THE MAP

Even the best strategies will fail if they are not communicated and executed. Many studies have shown that it is the organizations that have a common mind-set that win more consistently. A common mind-set means everyone in the organization knows what the strategy is and knows what tactics and plans to follow. Every employee should be able to clearly explain the strategy in a couple of sentences. They should be able to explain how they contribute to the strategy. When everyone can do that, you'll have achieved a common mind-set; you'll have reduced friction in your processes and increased the efficiency of decision making, resource allocation, and initiatives. Once a common mind-set is established, the rest depends on clear leadership and clean execution. Alignment is the operative word. All of the things the organization does need to align with the strategy. Policies should result in aligned behaviors. Rewards should support aligned behaviors. Processes and organizational structure need to be aligned. Deployment of leaders and teams needs to be aligned with and guided by the strategy. Total alignment leads to laser-like execution. Not a second wasted. Not a penny wasted. Mission accomplished.

SOME REMEDIES

1. **Focus.** Think laser—photons in a coherent beam. They're aligned. They're of one wavelength. They're focused. Bring a laser-like focus to everything. Your processes. Your organizational structure. Policies. Procedures. Compensation and rewards. Hiring. Performance management. Succession planning. Decision making. Communication. Everything focused on achieving your competitive business strategy.

2. **Communicate.** Communicate. Communicate. A common mind-set is created by communication and dialog. Think of it as a marketing campaign. If there was something very important for your customers to know, what would you do? Do the same with the strategy. Engage marketing professionals inside or outside the organization to create a marketing campaign complete with themes, slogans, ads, colors, and a communication strategy which includes multiple communication methods and channels. The dialog is for both understanding and ownership. Help people own the vision. Craft the message so it's crystal clear and easily under-stood by everyone. Embrace it passionately. Then, assuming you have the right people in the right roles, it's all about execution.

3. **Align with customers.** Design from the outside in. Start with the delighted customer. Design the distribution and delivery chain backwards, asking what each process step should look like to result in a delighted customer. What will the product look like? The service? What's the best way to get the order? The best way to deliver? Always think first of the customer.

21

4. **Align leadership.** Every strategy has a leadership brand that goes with it. Every strategy, given a particular industry context, location, and market, has a set of required leadership skills and competencies. A strategy that calls for speed in decision making needs speedy managers and executives. A strategy that calls for key account intimacy requires managers and executives that are good at forming lasting relationships. A strategy that calls for producing commodity products in a cost-conscious market needs leaders who are efficient managers. For each element of the strategy, consider what kind of a leader or manager will best be able to execute this element. Once you have the competencies, evaluate the current managers and executives and locate the fits and gaps. For the gaps, decide whether you will close the gap developmentally, find a better fit inside, or go outside to get the best fit.

5. **Align goals.** Common sense, right? Your top-level business objectives must align with your strategic intent. It starts at the top and cascades down to the individual employee. Every individual contributor should have goals aligned with and in support of the team. The team goals should be aligned with and in support of the department, and so forth. From the top of the organization to the bottom, establish goals so people and groups are aligned with the strategy.

6. **Align measurement.** Goals don't mean much if results aren't measured. Rigorously measure. Measure what matters to your strategy. Measurement gets people's attention. Measure inputs. Measure outputs. Measure processes. Use the results of measurement. Analyze, act, correct, change, improve. Make measurement and improvement part of everyone's job. Give them the tools and language and skills to measure effectively and to take corrective action for improvement.

7. **Align culture.** Culture is the way things are done in the organization, the sum of the habitual behaviors of the individuals. How do you hire? Promote? Celebrate? Make decisions? Reward? Communicate? Every organization has a certain style that may be more or less well defined. The style influences behavior. What behaviors do you need to support your strategy? What style will promote those behaviors? Choose a style, a culture that is aligned with your strategy, then adopt policies and procedures and an organizational structure that reflect that style. Model the behaviors you want emulated throughout the organization. Put structures in place to promote that culture. If you want a culture that drives decision making down to the lowest level, you need to have policies and procedures that empower frontline workers. That needs to become the norm. Talk it. Walk it. Reward it. Culture is a powerful influencer of organizational performance. Make it work for you.

8. **Give lots of feedback.** Feedback is an essential component of performance. Get employees aligned by communicating, goal setting, measurement, and also by including regular feedback on their performance. Effective feedback is specific,

22

direct, and delivered in a timely and genuine way by the manager or customer. Make your environment a feedback-rich environment, and supplement the feedback with coaching and mentoring to encourage and guide development in the core competencies.

9. **Align rewards.** Goals, measurement, feedback—all are essential components of aligned performance. Those are the things that get performance kick-started. But it is meaningful rewards and consequences that sustain the performance over the long haul. Align your reward system to your strategies to reinforce the behaviors, accomplishments, and skill development that will drive competitive advantage and success. The performance picture is not complete until you've aligned the rewards with your strategy.

10. **Align with best practices.** There are established and proven methods to improve business practices. Practices like Total Quality Management, Six Sigma, Lean Manufacturing, and Business Process Reengineering are all used to improve quality, productivity, timeliness, and costs associated with processes. Alignment with customers and strategy is inherently built into these practices. Consider these practices and adopt what best fits your organization. Pick something and get started.

SUGGESTED READINGS

Abraham, G. A. (2006). Strategic Alignment. *Leadership Excellence*, *23*(8), 12.

Allio, M. K. (2005). A short, practical guide to implementing strategy. *Journal of Business Strategy*, *26*(4), 12-21.

Aquila, A. J. (2005). Align compensation to your firm's strategic goals. *Accounting Today*, *19*(14), 9-23.

Bossidy, L., & Charan, R. (2002). *Execution: The discipline of getting things done.* New York, NY: Crown Business.

Bradford, R. (2002). Strategic alignment. *Executive Excellence*, *19*(1), 8-9.

Goodstein, L. D., Nolan, T. M., & Pfeiffer, J. W. (1993). *Applied strategic planning: A comprehensive guide.* New York: McGraw-Hill, Inc.

Gupta, A. K. (1984). Contingency linkages between strategy and general manager characteristics: A conceptual examination. *Academy of Management Review*, *9*, 399-412.

Gupta, A. K., & Govindarajan, V. (1984). Build, hold, harvest: Converting strategic intentions into reality. *Journal of Business Strategy*, *4*(3), 34-47.

Kaplan, R. S., & Norton, D. P. (2001). Building a strategy-focused organization. *Ivey Business Journal*, *65*(5), 12-19.

Kaplan, R. S., & Norton, D. P. (2006, March). How to implement a new strategy without disrupting your organization. *Harvard Business Review*, *84*(3), 100-109.

Kerr, J. L., & Jackofsky, E. F. (1989). Aligning managers with strategies: Management development versus selection. *Strategic Management Journal*, *10*, 157-170.

Lawler, E. (1996). *From the ground up: Six principles for building the new logic corporation.* San Francisco, CA: Jossey-Bass.

Steel, R. (1991). From paper to practice: Implementing the corporate strategic plan. *Business Quarterly, 55*(3), 119-124.

Williams, S. L. (2002). Strategic planning and organizational values: Links to alignment. *Human Resource Development International*, *5*(2), 217-233.

CLUSTER E: EXECUTION AND DECISION MAKING

Even if you're on the right track, you'll get run over if you just sit there.
Will Rogers – Humorist and social commentator

*Checking the results of a decision against its expectations
shows executives what their strengths are, where they need to improve,
and where they lack knowledge or information.*
Peter Drucker – Business theorist, author, and strategist

THE SIGNPOST

Executives execute. They make decisions and drive results. The value they provide is a function of the quality of those decisions and the speed at which they're made. Real-world business decisions are tough. There is never enough clarity, enough information, enough time for complete analysis and full identification of the risk factors. It's a wonder that good decisions can be made at all, but they are. Brilliant decisions are made consistently by skilled leaders who have clarity about the business strategy, have keenly developed analytical skills, business acumen, risk tolerance, and possess an intuitive grasp of context. The proof is in the pudding. Business successes, the results of sound decisions, tell the story. Fanatically promote and develop these competencies in your organization to be one of the winners.

ITEMS

5. Use our strategy to guide decision making
25. Make tough decisions quickly
45. Exhibit unrelenting and aggressive competitiveness in the marketplace
65. Execute and implement difficult strategies rapidly and effectively
83. Allocate proportionate resources to our most critical products and services

UNSKILLED

- Gets paralyzed by analysis; gets overwhelmed by data
- Doesn't make decisions aligned with the strategy
- Allows politics to dominate resource allocation decisions
- Moves too fast with insufficient consideration of risk factors
- Doesn't clearly or properly provide decision-making authority
- Is highly risk averse; terrified of making a mistake
- Has a roll-the-dice mentality; reckless and needless risk taking
- Fails to study and learn from mistakes
- Has judgment clouded by emotion; doesn't use data effectively

SKILLED

- Uses strategy considerations as major drivers in decision making
- Makes decisions as quickly as prudently possible
- Pushes decision-making authority as far down in the organization as is reasonable
- Tracks and studies decision results in order to improve
- Adopts formalized systems and processes for quick data acquisition and analysis
- Understands risk; adapts risk tolerance to match potential consequences, good and bad
- Embraces solutions that allow flexibility and accommodate post-decision adjustments
- Makes customers and financial implications part of every significant decision process
- Creates an organizational culture that encourages open debate; manages conflict well

SOME CAUSES

- Lack of focus; distraction
- Lethargy; lack of energy and urgency
- Reactive
- Lack of business acumen and analytical skills
- Tolerance for risk too low or too high
- Poor systems for data collection and analysis
- Timidity; lack of competitive drive
- Arrogance; unwillingness to learn from mistakes
- Lack of managerial courage

THE TEN LEADERSHIP ARCHITECT® COMPETENCIES MOST ASSOCIATED WITH THIS CLUSTER (in order of connectedness)

50. Priority Setting
12. Conflict Management
53. Drive for Results
51. Problem Solving
 1. Action Oriented
16. Timely Decision Making
32. Learning on the Fly
47. Planning
52. Process Management
58. Strategic Agility

E: EXECUTION & DECISIONS

DIMENSION II: STRATEGY EXECUTION

THE MAP

There are more good strategies and plans for action than there are examples of good plan execution. Most organizations can create strategies that, if implemented, would greatly enhance their performance. The majority of mergers and acquisitions fail due to poor execution of the plan. Most large-scale change efforts fail for the same reason. Getting the plan is just the battle begun. The real effort is in execution. Execution is probably a bigger differentiator than the plans. Most large organizations in the same industry have about the same strategic plans. They sound good. Who doesn't want to be the preferred investment? The preferred supplier? The employer of choice? Who doesn't aspire to compete globally? To be the first to market? To have the coolest products? To be the leader in customer service? Everyone thinks they're so unique, yet strategic goals look remarkably similar. The difference is in execution. Execution is hard work. It means paying attention. Never letting up. Attention to detail. Attention to data. Sound analysis. Risk considerations. Resource allocation. Conflict management. Accountability. Follow through. Speed. Courage. This is the meat and potatoes of management. Good decisions underpin execution. So do systems—financial, supply chain, human resources, sales and marketing, customer service. In everything, alignment is key. You can create a strategy in a weekend off-site workshop; it will take a year of hard work to execute it.

SOME REMEDIES

1. **Create a sense of urgency.** Without a sense of urgency, your organization will lumber along in a self-imposed stupor, stumbling over decisions and missing opportunities. You need to act out of a mix of paranoia and a competitive drive that charges everyone in your organization with energy and a focus on winning. Create a compelling vision of the world as it will be when you've achieved your strategic objectives. Contrast that with the world as it will be if you fail. Drive home the message with passion. It has to be genuine to be credible throughout the organization. The leadership team needs to really believe in the strategy, to want to win, to fear failure. If they believe it, they have a shot at selling it. When successful, that sense of urgency will spread through the organization like a contagion. No one will be satisfied with the status quo. Everyone will clamor for action. Urgency and a drive for results will become the norm in the organization's culture.

2. **Get fast.** Never underestimate the importance of speed. Speed drives customer satisfaction up and costs down. Speed drives the competition crazy. Be the first to recognize opportunities. Be the first to act on them. Adopt systems that improve timeliness and productivity. Ask for speed. Measure it. Reward it. Celebrate it. Teach it. Speak about it at every opportunity. Highlight case studies of speed. Speed is such a powerful competitive advantage that it deserves a prominent place in your strategy.

3. **Use a process.** Intuition has its place. It plays a part in decisions, sometimes a major role. But intuition can be a crutch and an excuse for a lack of business acumen and analytical ability. Big mistake. Adopt formal problem-solving and decision-making processes that are lean and practical. The processes should minimize in-basket time. Information should move quickly through the system to decision makers. Teach the processes at all levels. Challenge decision makers to explain the process they used to reach a decision. Develop methods to define decision thresholds based on the impact of the decision, good or bad. Financial hurdles are important thresholds but aren't the only ones to consider. Financial goals are just one part of your strategic plan. Incorporate your other strategic elements into the mix. Create guidelines for minimum data requirements. Often, organizations seek more than the optimal data and are late with a decision as a result. There should be a cost-benefit decision embedded in the larger decision to weigh the benefits of waiting for additional data against the costs associated with delaying.

4. **Allocate resources against the strategy.** Create a process for zero-based budgeting. Instead of basing next year's budget against an increase in this year's, start from zero against the strategy. Think of each year as a start-up with a new business plan. If there was no history and you had to go to capital markets for funds, what would you ask for? Where would you apply the resources? Make tough decisions. Shut things down that no longer play in the strategy. Start things up that weren't there last year. Reorganize against the strategy. Regroup against the strategy. Trim resources from some activities and significantly increase them in others. No sacred cows. No legacy activities. Start fresh.

5. **Get smart about the competition.** Create a formal competitive-intelligence process to learn about and track competitors. You can create a function, designate a task force, or hire an outside firm. But do something programmatic to study the competition. Consider creating a shadow management team to simulate your main competitors. Ask team members to play the roles of the competing CEOs and develop a game plan for competing against your organization. Report out on strategies. What have you learned? What insights into your competitor's strategies have you gained? Seek to get an understanding of your competitor's capabilities for execution. How do they compare to yours? In the end, determine how you can beat the competition through better execution.

6. **Embrace tough decisions.** Many organizations stall in the face of the tough decisions. They delay them. That's a mistake. Make the tough decisions first. Demonstrate courage in facing challenges. Be willing to take on the sacred cows, the things for which your organization holds an irrational affection that can't be easily explained or justified. What is sacred in your organization? If it doesn't support the strategy, if it doesn't serve the customer, it needs to be addressed. Don't be a prisoner of your history and legacy. A reputation for quality is a legacy that should be embraced and promoted. Other legacies aren't so desirable; they

can be downright nefarious. Slay the sacred cows that have it coming. Reward those who make the tough calls.

7. **Get serious about performance management.** Adopt best practices for performance management and use the system to promote execution of the strategic plan. Performance management starts with goal setting. Business objectives aligned with your strategic intent start at the top and cascade down through each level in the organization all the way to individual contributors so that everyone has meaningful stretch goals aligned with strategy. The goals form the basis for an ongoing dialogue between management and employees and an opportunity for feedback and coaching. At the end of the business cycle, performance is assessed against achievement of goals, against execution of the plan. The level of achievement, the measure of execution, should then be rewarded commensurately.

8. **Manage risk.** Develop methods for risk analysis and to define risk thresholds based on the impact of the decision, good or bad. Develop and continue to refine a process for setting confidence levels that are factored into decisions. Measure risk. Track your results. Modify your decision-making processes based on what you learn to improve results and reduce the time required to make decisions.

9. **Become a learning organization.** Learning is acquiring the ability to do something new, something different. Learning organizations adapt. They create knowledge, organize it, share it, and protect it. They are learning agile. They tolerate, even celebrate, mistakes because they treat them as an opportunity for learning. They have embedded knowledge management into their systems and embrace change. This is a profitable path to business success. Promote organizational learning with a passion.

10. **Drive individual development.** Your learning and development function should be aligned with and support the business strategy. The core competencies, including those above related to decision making and execution, should be at the centerpiece of training and development in the organization. Develop instruction around the systems and processes created to optimize execution. Teach analytical methods. Teach the business drivers for your organization. Teach problem-solving and decision-making techniques and involve employees in action-learning projects with real implications. Specifically teach the process of strategically guided decision making.

SUGGESTED READINGS

Altier, W. J. (1999). *The thinking manager's toolbox: Effective processes for problem solving & decision making*. New York, NY: Oxford University Press.

Bossidy, L., & Charan, R. (2002). *Execution: The discipline of getting things done*. New York, NY: Crown Business.

Bosssidy, L., & Charan, R. (2004). *Confronting reality: Doing what matters to get things right*. New York, NY: Crown Business.

Bridges, W. (2003). *Managing transitions: Making the most of change*. New York, NY: Perseus Books Group.

Conner, D. (1993). *Managing at the speed of change.* New York, NY: Random House.

Cox, G. (2000). *Ready-aim-fire problem solving: A strategic approach to innovative decision making*. Ireland: Oak Tree Press.

Drucker, P. F., Hammond, J., Keeney, R., Raiffa, H., & Hayashi, A. M. (Eds.). (2001). *Harvard Business Review on decision making*. Boston, MA: Harvard Business School Press.

Fogg, D. (1999). *Implementing your strategic plan: How to turn "intent" into effective action for sustainable change*. New York, NY: AMACOM.

Frigo, M. L. (2003). Strategy or execution? *Strategic Finance, 84*(9), 9-10.

Galpin, T. (1997). *Making strategy work: Building sustainable growth capacity*. San Francisco, CA: Jossey-Bass.

Gladwell, M. (2005). *Blink: The power of thinking without thinking*. New York, NY: Little, Brown and Company.

Hrebiniak, L. (2005). *Making strategy work: Leading effective execution and change*. Upper Saddle River, NJ: Wharton School Publishing.

Jones, M. (1998). *The thinker's toolkit: 14 Powerful techniques for problem solving*. New York, NY: Three Rivers Press.

Kaplan, R., & Norton, D. (1996). *The balanced scorecard: Translating strategy into action*. Boston, MA: Harvard Business School Press.

McAuliffe, T. (2005). *The 90% solution: A consistent approach to optimal business decisions*. Bloomington, IN: AuthorHouse.

Wall, S. J. (2004). *On the fly: Executing strategy in a changing world*. Hoboken, NJ: John Wiley & Sons, Inc.

Welch, D. A. (2001). *Decisions, decisions: The art of effective decision making*. Amherst, NY: Prometheus Books.

Welch, J., & Welch, S. (2005). *Winning*. New York, NY: HarperCollins Publisher, Inc.

E: EXECUTION & DECISIONS

DIMENSION II: STRATEGY EXECUTION

CLUSTER F: INNOVATION LEADERSHIP

Ideas won't keep; something must be done about them.
Alfred North Whitehead – Mathematician and philosopher

When you innovate, you've got to be prepared for everyone telling you you're nuts.
Larry Ellison – Founder and CEO, Oracle Corporation

THE SIGNPOST

Innovation is a key organizational capability. It's in short supply and difficult to develop. It means generating ideas—lots of ideas—and selecting from among them the best to develop, to drive through to full implementation. Successful organizations are like organisms that spawn a proliferation of ideas, incubate them, and then, importantly, execute to turn the ideas into new products and services that change the market. Your customers change. The competition changes. The world changes. Your organization must change, too, or suffer the fate of all organisms that don't adapt—extinction.

ITEMS

6. Know what and where to innovate
26. Innovate decisively and in a timely fashion
46. Leverage technology productively
66. Create breakthrough products and services

UNSKILLED

- Doesn't have an appetite for mistakes
- Fails to measure and reward innovation
- Doesn't use customer needs as the prime innovation driver
- Is highly risk averse
- Doesn't leverage new technologies
- Lacks a well-defined and systematic process for innovation management
- Underinvests in innovation
- Is complacent; rides successes for too long
- Is slow to make decisions
- Fails to recruit the right kind of talent

SKILLED

- Fosters a culture of experimentation and tolerance for mistakes
- Studies mistakes; sees everything as an opportunity for learning
- Places customer needs at the center of the innovation strategy
- Measures and rewards innovation with creative compensation incentives
- Effectively staffs and manages multifunctional, diverse teams
- Promotes curiosity and creative dissatisfaction with the status quo
- Follows a disciplined approach to R&D investments
- Has an unrelenting focus on getting ahead of the curve
- Embraces new technology and seeks practical applications
- Has a highly developed and appropriate tolerance for risk
- Supports formal and informal networks for knowledge sharing, learning, and innovation

SOME CAUSES

- Innovation strategy undefined or not aligned with business strategy
- Lack of creative talent
- Failure to listen
- Slow to change and act
- Lack of customer focus
- Low tolerance for ambiguity
- Technologically unsophisticated
- Lack of process orientation
- Complacency
- Dysfunctional culture

THE TEN LEADERSHIP ARCHITECT® COMPETENCIES MOST ASSOCIATED WITH THIS CLUSTER (in order of connectedness)

28. Innovation Management
51. Problem Solving
2. Dealing with Ambiguity
46. Perspective
50. Priority Setting
52. Process Management
32. Learning on the Fly
61. Technical Learning
33. Listening
15. Customer Focus

THE MAP

Creativity and innovation management are related but different. It takes both. Creativity is about idea generation. Lots and lots of ideas. It takes many ideas because most don't survive the progressive refinement required to get an idea to market. Innovation management creates and operates the idea filter, ensures financial discipline, serviceability, distribution, and the customer connection. Innovation management is rarely done by the same people who create the ideas. Highly creative people generally do not have the patience, political skills, and the process knowledge to move an idea through the complex maze created by the confluence of the organization and the marketplace. Innovators start by knowing which idea to push. Highly creative people generally never know which of their ideas will succeed. It's a partnership between the highly creative and the innovators. Innovation can result in huge killer applications that significantly alter existing markets, even create totally new markets as they kill others. Innovation can also be more subtle—just a small, incremental enhancement that is meaningful to the customer. Consider all the dimensions of enhancements that might be valued—cost, functionality, size, delivery channel, serviceability, environmental compatibility, speed, durability, and integration with other products/services. The list of potential product and service enhancements is endless, but all items on the list have something in common: They provide customers with some gain or spare them from some pain. Whatever your business, it's all about innovating to meet customer needs.

SOME REMEDIES

1. **Create an innovation strategy.** Define specific objectives for innovation that support your high-level business goals. Remember that innovation takes many forms and can impact products, services, processes, and more. Your innovation focus should be a direct reflection of your overall business goals and in complete alignment. Apply the same discipline around your innovation strategy as your business strategy. Incorporate goals, metrics, rewards, and communication. Design your organizational structure as required to support innovation teams and to facilitate the management of innovation—driving ideas to implementation.

2. **Shape a culture that promotes innovation.** Make innovation part of your culture by including innovation in mission statements, strategy documents, and visioning presentations. Craft a statement about innovation and the part it plays in making your organization more successful. Study how your more successful competitors position and use innovation to outmaneuver your efforts. Celebrate and highlight innovations. Innovative organizations have characteristics in common. Form a team to study the literature on innovative cultures. Report back to management. Select features of innovative cultures that would work in your organization. Form implementation teams for each aspect of culture. Put a member of the senior management team in charge. Simple things like listening, appreciative inquiry,

33

a tolerance for risk and failure might be some of those aspects. Cross-boundary information and idea sharing might be another. Tolerance for diverse viewpoints. Funding Skunk Works projects. Aggressive R&D. Customer intimacy. An informal environment. Open architecture. Select the elements of culture that work for you and implement them. Design your organizational structure to facilitate innovation. Make people and units responsible for innovation. Run innovation meetings. Communicate about innovation. Charter innovation teams. Initiate a suggestion system with specific criteria for innovative ideas from teams. Recognize and reward significant contributions. Embed innovation firmly in your culture.

3. **Become intimate with customer needs.** You first need to figure out what and where to innovate. That information resides in and around your customers. You need to know everything they want, need, and expect from your products and services. You need to understand the pain/gain factors. How can you ease their pain? Provide them some gain? Do surveys. Run focus groups. Visit key customers. Create customer advisory panels. Study customer behaviors. Check other parts of the world and other industries to see if there are innovations in other markets. Anticipate their future needs. Run customer scenarios about future needs and wants. Do trend analyses on your products and services. What's next? Anticipate solutions your customers haven't even yet realized they need. Knowing as much as possible about customer needs, desires, and expectations will give you the right focus for innovation.

4. **Define your innovation process.** Innovation management is a business process and should be defined and formalized just like other business processes. Start by defining outputs based on the customer requirements. Define the inputs and operations that add value to those inputs to create a suitable deliverable. How are ideas generated? Documented? Enhanced? Tested? What gates exist for moving ideas through to the next level? How do you fund development? When do you shelve an idea? How do you document what you're learning along the way? How do you share what you've learned? How are decisions made? Resources allocated? Where are the handoffs? How can the process be made more efficient, faster? What steps can be simplified? Eliminated entirely? What are the key roles? How should work be organized? There are many questions to answer, but they're well worth the time and effort if you want to avoid a haphazard and ineffective approach. Consider the TRIZ methodology for problem solving and practices from TQM and Six Sigma applied to your innovation process.

5. **Establish innovation metrics.** Measure innovation at the enterprise level. A common metric is the measure of cumulative profits generated from new products (a variation of ROI—return on innovation). You can also look at return on invested capital (ROIC). These are common financial measures, but don't limit your thinking to financial aspects. What is the impact of innovation on customer satisfaction? Employee engagement? Patent applications? Select the most appropriate metrics

and set goals that are achievable with a reasonable stretch component. Make the metrics visible and public. Revisit the metrics often to modify and add others as required. Put innovation metrics into the goals and measurements of functional business units and individuals, as well as at the enterprise level.

6. **Create incentives for innovation.** Apply innovation to incentives, too. Look for ways to drive increased innovation effectiveness through targeted reinforcement and rewards. Use a mix of tangible and intangible reinforcement—cash bonuses along with individualized intangibles. Make sure the link between achievement and reward is crystal clear, well communicated, and easily understood. Then, make sure you follow through without delay.

7. **Develop multifunctional innovation teams.** Innovation doesn't happen in a vacuum. It generally takes a diverse, multifunctional team with a mix of technical skills and wide-ranging abilities. You need the idea generators, the people who prolifically toss off new ideas with ease. You need people with intimate knowledge of the customer. You need engineering and marketing expertise. You need project managers, financial analysts, and designers. The successful team will share a commitment and sense of ownership for the team goals, trust each other, hold each other accountable, and manage the conflict that is inherent in any workgroup.

8. **Create innovation networks for knowledge sharing and learning.** Make studying innovation a part of the knowledge base of your organization. Create groups to study various aspects of innovation and report back to management with recommendations about how it might work for you. Study the best. Study your competitors. Look outside your area to study innovation in areas such as art, music, and architecture. Invite innovation experts to address management and innovation teams. Consider how an innovation consultant might help. Share the results of all of these projects widely. Summarize the lessons learned. Create internal innovation networks and promote participation in networks that extend beyond the organization. "Open Innovation" is a term promoted by Henry Chesbrough, a professor and executive director at the Center for Open Innovation at Berkeley. The idea behind open innovation is that in a global world of widely distributed knowledge, individual companies cannot afford to rely entirely on their own innovation. Organizations should, in addition to their own efforts, buy or license innovations from other companies. In the past, companies tended to keep their discoveries highly secret and made little attempt to assimilate information from outside. Major advances in electronic technology have facilitated the easy exchange of information. So easy that it seems sometimes impossible to prevent. Innovative organizations tend to look outside for innovation in addition to their homegrown ideas. They also tend to export their own innovations through partnerships and alliances.

DIMENSION III: MANAGING INNOVATION AND CHANGE

F: INNOVATION LEADERSHIP

9. **Hire and develop the right talent.** In addition to technical and business expertise, you need to have creative talent and innovation managers. People who are creative can tend toward the eccentric. It's the nature of the creative process. Hiring and managing creative people present special challenges. You cannot have innovation without the ideas. The ideas will not do you any good without the managers of innovators. They have the skill sets to effectively determine how to allocate resources, and then to shepherd the innovation project through the organization and out to the market. Recruit a mix of people who have passion and a competency profile for creativity and for innovation management. If your organization is having difficulty with innovation, use the ten competencies listed above to enhance those skills internally. Put those ten competencies into all your talent management processes—including your 360° process, into your performance management system, into your hiring and staffing process, and into succession management. Develop the competencies relentlessly. Create coursework around innovation. Select innovation programs from outside your organization for people to attend. Hire innovation coaches.

10. **Apply fiscal discipline to innovation.** Financial metrics have been suggested above, but this is an area that deserves special emphasis. To begin, you need to determine what to budget for R&D to meet your strategic goals. The commitment of resources is important; you are, in essence, purchasing the future. Skimp on resources devoted to innovation and you'll mortgage your future to enhance current performance. Study the annual reports of other businesses in your industry to see what percent of revenue they're devoting to R&D. How do you measure up? That's one issue. Another is how the budget is managed once the commitment is made. R&D becomes a black hole in many organizations into which resources are poured and then seemingly disappear. There is often a different level of financial control and discipline exercised in the R&D function. This is a mistake. The same rigor applied to manufacturing should be applied to innovation. Be clear about financial hurdles at each decision gate in your innovation process.

SUGGESTED READINGS

Barker, J. (1992). *Future edge: Discovering the new paradigms of success.* New York, NY: William Morrow & Company.

Barker, J. (2005). *Five regions of the future: Preparing your business for tomorrow's technology future.* New York, NY: Penguin Group.

Brown, S., & Eisenhardt, K. (1998). *Competing on the edge.* Boston, MA: Harvard Business School Press.

Carlson, C., & Wilmot, W. (2006). *Innovation: The five disciplines for creating what customers want.* New York, NY: Crown Business.

Chakravorti, B. (2003). *The slow pace of fast change: Bringing innovations to market in a connected world.* Boston, MA: Harvard Business School Press.

Chesbrough, H. (2003). *Open innovation: The new imperative for creating and profiting from technology.* Boston, MA: Harvard Business School Press.

Chesbrough, H. (2006). *Open business models: How to thrive in the new innovation landscape.* Boston, MA: Harvard Business School Press.

Chesbrough, H., Vanhaverbeke, W., & West, J. (Eds.). (2006). *Open innovation: Researching a new paradigm.* New York, NY: Oxford University Press.

Christensen, C. M. (1997). *The innovator's dilemma.* Boston, MA: Harvard Business School Press.

Davila, T., Epstein, M. J., & Shelton, R. (2006). *Making innovation work: How to manage it, measure it, and profit from it.* Upper Saddle River, NJ: Wharton School Publishing.

Deschamps, J. (2005). Different leadership skills for different innovation strategies. *Strategy & Leadership, 33*(5), 31-38.

Elenkov, D. S., & Manev, I. M. (2005). Top management leadership and influence on innovation. The role of sociocultural context. *Journal of Management, 31*(3), 381-402.

Gebert, D., Boerner, S., & Lanwehr, R. (2003). The risks of autonomy: Empirical evidence for the necessity of a balance management in promoting organizational innovativeness. *Creativity and Innovation Management, 12*(1), 41-49.

Govindarajan, V., & Trimble, C. (2005). *Ten rules for strategic innovators: From idea to execution.* Boston, MA: Harvard Business School Press.

Hesselbein, F., Goldsmith, M., & Sommerville, I. (2001). *Leading for innovation and organizing for results.* San Francisco, CA: Jossey-Bass.

Krause, D. E. (2004). Influence-based leadership as a determinant of the inclination to innovation and of innovation-related behaviors: An empirical investigation. *Leadership Quarterly, 15*(1), 79-102.

Kuczmarski, T. (1988). The ten traits of an innovation mindset. *Journal of Quality & Participation, 21*(6), 44-46.

Mansfield, E. (1985). How rapidly does new industrial technology leak out? *Journal of Industrial Economics, 34*(2), 217–223.

Mumford, M. D., & Licuanan, B. (2004). Leading for innovation: Conclusion, issues, and directions. *Leadership Quarterly, 15*(1), 163-171.

Rickards, T., & Moger, S. (2006). Creative leaders: A decades of contribution from creativity and innovation management journal. *Creativity and Innovation Management, 15*(1), 4-18.

Sloane, P. (2003). *The leader's guide to lateral thinking skills: Powerful problem-solving techniques to ignite your team's potential.* London, UK: Kogan Page.

Smith, G. P. (1996). *The new leader: Bringing creativity and innovation to the workplace.* Delray Beach, FL: St. Lucie Press.

Sternberg, R. J., Kaufman, J. C., & Pretz, J. E. (2004). A propulsion model of creative leadership. *Creativity and Innovation Management, 13*(3), 145-153.

Utterback, J. M., Suarez, F. F. (1993). Innovation, competition, and industry structure. *Research Policy 22*(1), 1–21.

von Hippel, E. (2005). *Democratizing innovation.* Cambridge, MA: MIT Press.

CLUSTER G: ORGANIZATIONAL LEARNING

We are not what we know but what we are willing to learn.
Mary Catherine Bateson – Writer and cultural anthropologist

*An organization's ability to learn, and translate that learning
into action rapidly, is the ultimate competitive advantage.*
Jack Welch – Former Chairman and CEO, General Electric

THE SIGNPOST

Learning is acquiring the ability to do something new, something different. Learning organizations adapt. They create knowledge, organize it, enhance it, share it, and protect it. They are learning agile. They have embedded knowledge management into their systems and embrace change.

ITEMS

7. Generate new ways to do things
27. Freely discard and change policies, practices, and processes to respond to new challenges
47. Generalize and transfer critical knowledge and ideas seamlessly across boundaries and between units, functions, and geographies inside the organization
67. Have a well-supported process and culture of challenging the status quo
84. Generate impactful ideas through experimentation, continuous improvement, or benchmarking
91. Rapidly and effectively adjust to crises, economic turmoil, natural disasters, acts of terrorism, and other unanticipated disruptions

UNSKILLED

- Avoids the pain and difficulty of change
- Is weighed down by legacy, by the past
- Is organized with silos and roadblocks that stifle learning
- Doesn't support risk; punishes failure
- Doesn't study failures; repeats mistakes
- Is slow to adjust to disruptive events
- Is technologically inept; is slow to adopt and apply new technologies
- Squelches bad news and kills the messenger so that upward information is chilled and filtered
- Doesn't look outside itself for help

39

- Is averse to critical feedback from inside or outside
- Has management that is insulated, imperial, and distant
- Is reactive; doesn't consider and plan for a range of business scenarios

SKILLED

- Values and rewards learning from all sources
- Embraces change enthusiastically; easily adapts to changes in the environment
- Maintains a broad perspective to proactively identify problems, opportunities, and solutions
- Fosters exploration and experimentation
- Tolerates mistakes, studies them, learns from them
- Institutionalizes knowledge management with systems and processes
- Demonstrates prudence but is not afraid of taking risks
- Is free from baggage of the past
- Tolerates criticism from inside and outside; seeks feedback
- Deals comfortably with ambiguity and stress
- Institutionalizes change management practices
- Promotes diversity of ideas, styles, backgrounds, and viewpoints

SOME CAUSES

- Risk aversion
- Mired in the past
- Insulated and closed to outside ideas
- Narrow perspective
- Complacency
- Procrastination
- Lack of diversity
- Indecisive
- Turnover too low

THE TEN LEADERSHIP ARCHITECT® COMPETENCIES MOST ASSOCIATED WITH THIS CLUSTER (in order of connectedness)

2. Dealing with Ambiguity
12. Conflict Management
51. Problem Solving
32. Learning on the Fly
33. Listening
9. Command Skills
52. Process Management
1. Action Oriented
40. Dealing with Paradox
57. Standing Alone

THE MAP

You can't get better without change, without doing something new and different. That's what learning is all about. The advantage of being a learning organization in a time of near-chaotic change is clear. Being a learning organization requires that individuals within that organization be learning agile and adaptable. It's impossible to conceive of a learning organization comprised of individuals who are nonlearners. It's difficult to conceive of an organization full of learning-agile and adaptable people that is not a learning organization. It is a complex dance between the collective characteristics of individuals and the organization's culture and operating tone. Seems people were really not built for change. They naturally seek predictability, consistency, comfort, habit, security, and routine. People prefer to stay in their comfort zones. In the midst of chaos, organizations likewise tend to seek stability, order, structure, predictability. They find it easiest to move slowly, deliberately, to prefer the status quo. But change isn't optional. Successful organizations are nimble, lean, adaptable. They morph into what they need to be. They change on a dime—and like it! Customers have grown to expect it. Customers are more demanding, less loyal, and seek instant gratification. Customers have an ever-widening array of options and sources. To be successful in this environment, organizations must be adaptable. They must be learning agile.

SOME REMEDIES

Note: *Being a learning organization is a well-known and researched state. Peter Senge, Cal Wick, and others over the years have explored what it means to become a learning organization. Many organizations have paid attention and now have a new position to oversee learning—the CLO (chief learning officer). The tips that follow are heavily dependent upon the work of Senge, Wick, and others who have followed their lead.*

1. **Take a systems approach.** One of the keys to understanding change is knowing how things fit together. There is a field of study called systems theory which views organizations as interconnected parts that work together to create entirely new properties in the whole. In systems theory, all things move together. If you tweak one part of the system, it moves other parts. If you concentrate on increasing revenue, margins may erode. If you concentrate on increasing cash flow, revenue may degrade. If you make deep discount deals exclusively with key customers, the rest of your customers will revolt. If you invest in one plant, the others will fall behind. Systems theory also speaks to archetypes. These are repeating patterns that can be used to analyze, predict, and, in some cases, impact outcomes. Some of these archetypes have moved into the common vernacular. The statement "no good deed goes unpunished" describes a repeating pattern of group behavior. What is deemed a good act by one will be lost on another and misinterpreted as negative by yet another. Another archetype is called the "tragedy of the commons." In this archetype, a seemingly good idea—for example, putting shared resources into a central pool and then dispensing services across the

DIMENSION III: MANAGING INNOVATION AND CHANGE

G: ORGANIZATIONAL LEARNING

enterprise in an effort to save money—turns out to be very difficult. Typically, customer satisfaction goes down when resources are pooled. Few get the service they experienced before. Another archetype that comes into play in this example is "resources to the resourceful." According to this pattern, the resourceful get a disproportionate share of resources at the expense of the less resourceful. Systems theory needs to be part of the knowledge base of learning organizations. It needs to be taught in the learning center. Experts need to be brought in to speak to management. It needs to be considered in annual strategic planning sessions. Those ignorant of history are destined to repeat it. Those unaware of systems theory will be left behind.

2. **Know thyself.** Learning for individuals starts with self-knowledge, with acknowledgement of the need to learn and then knowing what to learn. Learning requires acceptance of feedback and the self-confidence to accept that current knowledge and skills are incomplete. It's no different for entire enterprises. Being a learning organization starts with a culture, a collective attitude that admits it doesn't know everything, that admits there is more to learn, that understands that not all answers reside inside. This culture seeks to find answers wherever they may be. How does an entire enterprise get feedback? By being open about its faults and by inviting feedback internally and externally. It's basic listening. An enterprise needs feedback from employees, customers, shareholders, and other constituencies. The more the better. It has to know what it's not doing well. Invite dialog. Be open. Make sure top management gets a healthy flow of input. Celebrate flaws as opportunities for learning.

3. **Promote learning collaboration.** Another feature of a learning organization is a shared mind-set about learning. In the learning organization, everyone shares a vision about where the organization wants to go and, generally, how it will get there. Everyone is on the same path and open to the new, the different, and the improved. People share a passion for that vision. Their shared mind-set includes a willingness to learn. It includes a commitment to openness, to listening. The shared mind-set is best set collectively through open dialog and problem solving. It needs to be well communicated and translated into day-to-day behaviors. Weave the necessity for and willingness to learn into the fabric of the enterprise.

4. **Think freely.** To be a learning organization, the thinking stream needs to be clear of biases, unsupported assumptions, prejudices, preconceived conclusions, and inappropriate advocacy. The nature of the thinking and decision-making process needs to be open dialog that is free of personalized arguments and power-based preferences. Organizations with noisy and filtered thinking and decision-making processes default to those in power. If the powerful are always right, it works. If they are human, it doesn't. Work on the nature of the thinking and decision-making processes in the organization. Work with individual leaders on facilitation

skills. Learn about the technique of appreciative listening. Use Edward de Bono's *Six Thinking Hats.* Give everyone feedback about their behavior in decision-making settings. Teach appreciative inquiry in the learning center. Have a real commitment to the unvarnished truth.

5. **Model learning.** It is much easier to have a learning organization if you have learning leaders as models. Some research has shown that as leaders move to the top, they actually listen less and depend upon themselves more. Use the ten competencies listed above as a guide to enhance the learning willingness and ability of leaders. Work on the learning agility of the people at the top so they can model learning behaviors.

6. **Look outside.** "Open Innovation" is a term promoted by Henry Chesbrough, a professor and executive director at the Center for Open Innovation at Berkeley. The idea behind open innovation is that in a global world of widely distributed knowledge, individual companies cannot afford to rely entirely on their own innovation. In the past, companies made little attempt to assimilate information from outside. But today, companies benchmark other companies. Use consultants. Bring in outside speakers. Form groups of people who are new and fresh to the organization for input. Bring in customers. Use technology to facilitate learning through expert networks and directories, instant messaging, e-learning portals, coaching and mentoring networks, knowledge management systems, etc.

7. **Employ purposeful forgetting.** C.K. Prahalad was asked his opinion about the learning organization. He said most of the organizations he worked with as a top strategy consultant had no trouble learning. He said their bigger problem was forgetting. He makes the point that in order to do the new, you have to get rid of the old. Many organizations have trouble making room for the new. They hang on to legacy too long, on to what has worked in the past, what they did before. The GE Workout program was, in part, an attempt to get rid of things that no longer worked. Programs like Six Sigma, TQM, and business process reengineering all help clear out the old and dysfunctional. If your organization doesn't use one of those programs, create one that fits your organization. Be on the hunt for things from the past that are getting in the way of learning. Make it okay to question the relevance of existing rules and policies. Celebrate learning. Respect the past but don't be trapped by it.

8. **Seek best targets.** A learning organization needs to be selective about what it seeks to learn. It must find the right opportunities. Unbridled learning may not be the best process to follow. Might be as bad as no learning at all. Organizations need to be constantly scanning to find the areas in which they will most benefit from fresh thinking. Well-run organizations strike a balance between stability and renewal, between maintenance and creation. They look to the future while considering the past and present. A learning organization has to have a scanning

process to find targets, to follow trends, to keep an eye on the competition. Talk to customers. Listen inside and outside. Read and listen to leading thinkers. Look for opportunities. Detect flaws and breakdowns.

9. **Learn through people.** Typically, about one-third of learning is through others. Collective people skills in the organization can either enable or chill learning. Learning is give-and-take. Learning is tolerating. Patience and listening. Sharing. Freedom to ask. Deferring to others. Delegating. Learning is respect for others. Efficient, well-run meetings. Speaking up. Working through conflicts. So a learning-agile organization must have above-average people skills. Make sure people skills are in all of the talent management systems—performance management, recruiting profiles, development protocols, courses in the learning center, and succession planning. Make sure people skills are included in the goals of individual development plans. Create a feedback-rich environment and freely give individuals feedback on their people skills. Make sure people skills are mentioned in the strategic and value documents.

10. **Follow through.** Learning organizations never leave an event or complete a project—good or bad—without debriefing what worked and what didn't. They learn from successes and failure. They carry the learnings forward to apply to future situations. Institutionalize postmortem meetings and make sure you have recording and communication systems to capture and disseminate organizational learnings. Make them part of the stories of the culture.

44

SUGGESTED READINGS

Argyris, C., & Schön, D. (1978). *Organizational learning: A theory of action perspective*. Reading, Mass: Addison Wesley.

Argyris, C., & Schön, D. (1996). *Organizational learning II: Theory, method and practice*. Reading, Mass: Addison Wesley.

Bolman, L. G., & Deal, T. E. (1997). *Reframing organizations: Artistry, choice and leadership* (2nd ed.). San Francisco, CA: Jossey-Bass.

Chesbrough, H. (2006). *Open business models: How to thrive in the new innovation landscape*. Boston, MA: Harvard Business School Press.

Chesbrough, H., Vanhaverbeke, W., & West, J. (Eds.). (2006). Open innovation: *Researching a new paradigm*. New York, NY: Oxford University Press Inc.

Cohen, D., & Prusak, L. (2001). *In good company: How social capital makes organizations work*. Boston, MA: Harvard Business School Press.

De Bono, E. (1999). *Six thinking hats*. Boston, MA: Back Bay Books.

Marquardt, M. J. (2002). *Building the learning organization* (2nd ed.). Mountain View, CA: Davies-Black Publishing.

Marquardt, M. J., & Reynolds, A. (1993). *The global learning organization*. Chicago, IL: Irwin Professional Publishing.

Robinson, G., & Wick, C. (1992). *Executive development that makes a difference*. Human Resource Planning, *15*(1), 63-77.

Scholtes, P. (1997). The leaders handbook: *Making things happen, getting things done*. New York, NY: McGraw-Hill.

Senge, P. (1990). *The fifth discipline: The art and practice of the learning organization*. New York, NY: Random House.

Senge, P., Kleiner, A., Roberts, C., Ross, R. B., & Smith, B. J. (1994). *The fifth discipline fieldbook: Strategies and tools for building a learning organization*. New York, NY: Currency.

Tsang, E. (1997). Organizational learning and the learning organization: A dichotomy between descriptive and prescriptive research. *Human Relations*, *50*(1), 57-70.

Watkins, K., & Marsick, V. (Eds.). (1993). *Sculpting the learning organization: Lessons in the art and science of systematic change*. San Francisco, CA: Jossey-Bass.

Wick, C. (1996). *The learning edge*. New York, NY: McGraw-Hill.

Wick, C., Pollock, R., Jefferson, A., Flanagan, R., & Wilde, K. (2006). *The six disciplines of breakthrough learning: How to turn training and development into business results*. San Francisco, CA: Pfeffer.

CLUSTER H: UPGRADING THE WORKFORCE

We need to make sure we have the best people we can in our operations,
and that is a constant challenge. There is always room to improve.
James Packer – Executive Chairman, PBL, Australian media company

Treat people as if they were what they ought to be
and you help them to become what they are capable of being.
Johann Wolfgang Goethe – German poet, novelist, scientist, and painter

THE SIGNPOST
There's a war for talent that's going to intensify as baby boomers move into retirement. What will it take to identify and attract the best talent, to get them aligned, keep them motivated, and entice them to stay? Successful organizations will figure it out sooner and do it better than all the rest.

ITEMS
8. Continuously upgrade our workforce by bringing in new talent, keeping the best, and releasing the lowest performers
28. Have a well-supported process in place to orient new employees to our culture
48. Invest in building existing talent through training, development, and work experiences
68. Promote the right people
85. Have a feedback-rich environment in which everyone knows where he or she stands

UNSKILLED
- Is a poor judge of talent; fails in hiring and promotion decisions
- Compromises on talent; makes do with less than the best
- Has top management that is not fully engaged in the talent management process
- Is ineffective at integrating new people into the organization
- Fails to implement best talent management practices
- Wastes training resources on ineffective programs and methods
- Doesn't proactively engage in succession management
- Has dysfunctional culture; structures, policies, and practices hinder performance
- Fails to implement an effective performance management system

- Tolerates marginal performers; doesn't differentiate performance
- Is ineffective in providing performance feedback
- Fails to provide employees the tools, materials, and guidance to do the job

SKILLED

- Accurately appraises performance; applies differential treatment to high and low performers
- Deals with low performers compassionately but firmly; removes chronic underperformers
- Implements best practices in talent management
- Studies and adopts practices of recognized best places to work
- Fosters a feedback-rich culture infused with actionable, timely, and candid feedback for all
- Pays attention to employee integration; implements a comprehensive on-boarding process
- Implements a rigorous performance management system
- Is committed to finding and hiring the best
- Is committed to providing growth and development opportunities to all
- Allocates resources effectively to ensure the environment supports optimum performance
- Accurately assesses talent; assesses learning agility in succession management
- Passionately builds a high-performance culture that hires, develops, and promotes the best

SOME CAUSES

- Lack of managerial courage
- Low performance standards
- Lack of sophistication about talent and people
- Impatient culture
- Short-term mentality
- Boring business proposition
- Inadequate development of people strategy
- Insufficient resources devoted to talent management
- Disruptive history
- Unattractive geography
- Favoritism and/or nepotism

THE TEN LEADERSHIP ARCHITECT® COMPETENCIES MOST ASSOCIATED WITH THIS CLUSTER (in order of connectedness)

56. Sizing Up People

13. Confronting Direct Reports

12. Conflict Management

27. Informing

33. Listening

36. Motivating Others

19. Developing Direct Reports and Others

58. Strategic Agility

25. Hiring and Staffing

35. Managing and Measuring Work

THE MAP

People are our most important assets. Our most important assets walk out the door every evening. How often have you heard these platitudes? Are they true? Do top-notch people make a difference? In a word, yes! It's true. It's well documented. Virtually every study that has been conducted has concluded that the organizations with the highest caliber talent win. Workforce quality can provide a major competitive edge. So what does it mean to have the best people? It means that today I have the best-skilled people in every position—my people know how to do their jobs better than the competition's people. It means that my people are better managed than the competition's people—it doesn't do much good to have skilled people in the jobs if they're badly managed. It means that I have a productive and supportive culture for those great mangers and best people to work in. People receive the resources they need to perform their jobs. They have access to training and information. Obstacles are removed. Bureaucracy is minimized. People management systems make sense and are equitable. Taken together, this means the organization's a great place to work. It has great managers who have great people. There is an engaging business proposition. It's interesting. It's challenging. It's worthy of employees' time and effort. It means that the strategy, mission, and business proposition are well communicated and understood by all. To attract and retain great managers and people, you need great leaders with great people skills. And you need them now. To ensure your future, work to create internal capability to develop leaders for the future. People stay with organizations that have a great future. So upgrading the workforce involves addressing a number of issues and taking considerable actions. Taken together, they will help the organization succeed now and in the future. It's a closed loop. Great places to work attract great people. Great people create great places to work. Great people create engaging businesses and productive cultures. Engaging businesses attract talent. Talent plans for the future. It all works together.

H: UPGRADING WORKFORCE DIMENSION IV: ATTRACTING/RETAINING/MOTIVATING TALENT

SOME REMEDIES

1. **Keep your eye on the prize.** At the top of the organization, upgrading talent has to be front and center. Bake the talent mind-set into everything. Make the business case for talent management; establish the ROI of upgrading the workforce. If necessary, educate top management on the importance and ROI of talent management. As a start, read all of Professor Mark Huselid's work. Just Google his Web site. Make talent management a key element in the organization's vision and mission statements. Have a talent management plan as a subset of the strategic plan. Set goals for talent management and put them into incentive plans. Evaluate managers against them. Require top managers to work the importance of talent management into their speeches.

2. **Create a feedback-rich environment.** The research is clear. Self-awareness is one of the main drivers of success. People who know themselves better are more successful. People improve on weaknesses just by receiving candid, actionable feedback. People need feedback to grow and develop. Not knowing where I stand is one of the bottom-third rated items on most morale and engagement surveys. Most performance rating distributions are weighted toward the high end. More than 70% of people are rated at meets expectations or higher. Most people get inflated, less-than-complete feedback. It's common in exit interviews connected to involuntary turnover for the terminated employees to claim they had never been told their performance was not meeting expectations. The feedback-rich environment should be built from the top. Few top managers actually get performance reviews. When they do, they aren't meaningful because they're inflated. Ratings tend to be high. Rosy. Glowing. Those highly rated people then turn around and rate their people high, and so the disservice is perpetuated throughout the organization. It's just the easy way for spineless managers to check off the appraisal from the list of unpleasant management tasks and to avoid difficult discussions. How much better to have a feedback-rich environment? An environment in which feedback is given freely and received with an open mind. Feedback that is candid, timely, and actionable. To be candid, it has to be true. Start a campaign. Start it at the top. A campaign to give more candid and critical feedback. Require performance evaluation grades to be distributed or rank ordered. Require managers to spread out their ratings. Make sure feedback is balanced with at least as much critical and constructive feedback as positive. Use 360° techniques. Anonymous feedback tends to be more accurate than face-to-face.

3. **Deploy best people practices.** There are many pieces and parts to the people management system. From recruiting to retirement planning. In between there are many systems that touch people's lives and careers. Performance management. Career development. Succession planning. Benefits. Compensation. Training. Feedback. Coaching. Staffing. Team building. For each, there is a set of best practices agreed upon by both academics and practitioners. Learn the best practices that best fit your organization. Do an audit of your people processes and systems. Address the gaps.

4. **Use science to build the people future.** An important part of long-term upgrading is the talent management and succession planning systems. The process is straightforward. Select a subset of your employee population that you think has the potential for significant growth. We can call them high potentials. Apply the necessary developmental resources to help them grow and develop over time on their way to a senior assignment. Make sure that from an actuarial standpoint, there is an adequate supply of high potential candidates to fill the open jobs in the future. Easily said. Each of these simple steps has bumps in the road. Identifying high potentials is easier said than done. It is very difficult for most managers. There are two major barriers. The first is attitudinal. Identifying high potentials is an elitist activity. It's based upon the assumption that some people are better than others. A lot of managers and organizations have trouble with that. It also assumes that not everyone will make it. That flies in that face of egalitarian development for everyone. Study after study has shown that the unwillingness to face up to the difficult task of differentiating and separating the high potentials from the rest is a very success-limiting factor. The second deterrent is the difficulty of accuracy in high-potential identification. For this, we have science. There are now multiple studies of the characteristics of high potentials. There are questionnaires that managers can use to help them identify the right people. Assisted identification is the answer to this challenge—managerial judgment combined with science.

5. **Promote the right people.** There are two basic reasons to put someone in a new job: The first is to get that job done; the second is to expose someone to something new to develop his or her skills on the way to greater responsibility in the future. The first reason considers the job first. Generally, the best person is someone who has done that or a similar job well in the past. So if the job were a start-up, it would be best to put someone in that job who has had successful start-up experience. The second reason considers development first. Most organizations balk at putting people in jobs for the purpose of development. By definition, it will be someone who hasn't done that or similar jobs before, at least not well. The goal in a developmental fill is twofold. One is to get the job done as well as is possible, considering that the person hasn't done it before. The second

51

is to expose that person to the elements in that job which will put him or her in a better position to lead in the future. Now, there is some good news. The nature of high potentials is that they are able to perform under first-time conditions. That is, compared to those with less potential, high potentials will get off to a better start and will do better in the job, maybe not as well as someone who has done that exact job successfully before, but well enough. So if you select the right person (see tip above), then the risks associated with putting people into jobs for the purpose of development are reduced.

6. **Cull the poorest performers.** Upgrading can be done in three ways. First, you can bring in good people, people better than the ones you have. That increases the average skill per person. Second, you can develop the people you have. You can help them perform better. You can apply resources to help them grow and develop. That increases the average skill per person. The fastest but the hardest way is to release the bottom performers. That increases the skills per person in the people remaining. Firing is tough; it carries a lot of emotion and guilt. Being able to do that comfortably is in the bottom ten skills of most managers. Group layoffs are often easier than releasing one person at a time. We all know the impact of one person who is not pulling his or her weight. The rest have to work harder to compensate. Bad bosses and bad people take a big bite out of morale. Not bad in the sense of lying, cheating, and stealing, but bad in the sense of unproductive attitude and not carrying their weight. The old saying that one bad apple can spoil the barrel is true. One employee with a poor attitude or low performance can impact many others. Identify the laggards. Give them candid, timely, and actionable feedback. Put them on a short improvement plan. Provide all of the help that is practical. Closely monitor their progress. If there isn't a meaningful change, take decisive action. Institutionalize the practice of letting those bottom performers go. Help managers build the case. Help managers with the tough conversations. Have the HR and legal functions lay out the process. Enlist many to work on it together. Have every department and work unit begin to assess performance more accurately, releasing the chronic low performers and then hiring people better than the ones that leave. The average performance will increase rapidly. Make releasing the bottom a normal part of managing. Hold managers accountable. Provide the support. It's not easy or nice, but it is necessary.

7. **Integrate employees with an effective on-boarding process.** One part of upgrading is to help people get off to a good start. A significant percentage of people taking new jobs stumble or even fail. Many more get off to a slow start. There are many reasons for the stumble. They may not be truly qualified. In this case, the person or persons making the hiring or promotion decision made a bad call. There could be incorrect specifications about the job requirements or a failure to identify softer requirements, variables such as values or personality. Cultural

rejection is another reason for problems. In this case, the person is qualified from a job content standpoint but his or her style, values, attitudes, or other personal characteristics don't fit the existing culture, and the current workgroup members formally or informally conspire to sabotage the new person's experience. There might be poorly set expectations about the job. The new employee finds the particular job isn't what was expected and loses motivation or never gets engaged at all. There can also be problems from poorly set expectations about the organization. The employee has certain expectations, about career opportunities, for instance, and discovers the company can't deliver on those expectations. There can be problems due to a bad boss—bad in the sense of a mismatch between employee and boss styles or personalities. Even if none of these specific problems apply, new employees may fail simply due to the organization's inattention to the integration process. Management attention is required to integrate employees into the social and work systems. People coming from the outside stumble and fail at a higher rate than people placed into new positions from inside the organization. Mistakes are costly regardless of the cause. Experts put the cost somewhere between three to six times the fully burdened annual salary of the employee. The failure rate depends upon the position level and other factors, but it's a good estimate that between 25% and 50% of new employees at least stumble on new jobs, with some lesser percentage failing totally and leaving prematurely. Successful on-boarding is a four-step process. Step one is pre-start preparation. Getting a person better prepared before the start date will increase the chances of a good beginning. Have someone knowledgeable (usually the boss or unit HR person) spend a day off-site with the incoming person reviewing everything about the job, the workgroup, the context, the culture, the history and the mission, vision, and strategy of the organization. The second step is integration and assimilation, which usually takes about 90 days. It's in this period that first impressions are formed. As the saying goes, "You can't make a first impression twice." Assign a guide or orienteer to the incoming person. Formally schedule an opportunity to meet and have meaningful conversations with peers and coworkers. Create a network for the person. Assign a mentor if you have such a program. Have the boss work particularly hard on inclusion and informing. Track progress. Consider assigning an outside on-boarding coach. There are many firms that have on-boarding coaches, and there are on-boarding software applications to help manage the process. Do everything you can to get them off to the best start possible. The third step is engagement. After the person gets off to a good start, then for the next nine months concentrate on getting them invested in and passionate about the organization and its mission. Arrange meetings with members of top management so the employee can hear about the vision. Have them do a deep dive into the strategy. Finally, the last step is retention. After the first year, you should have a good feel about whether you want this person as part

53

of the organization long-term. If the answer is yes, then create a retention plan custom designed for the person. What elements of the work and organization will keep this person over the long-term? Put them in place.

8. **Become a best place to work.** The secret is out. We know what factors employees identify as important in organizations identified as being a best place to work. Several business publications publish annual rankings of the best places to work. And there are associated studies outlining the best practices that go along with being one of the best places. Study the lists. Examine the studies. Create a checklist for your organization. Do an audit. Act as if you were going to compete to get on one of the lists. Look to the gaps. Form workgroups around each of the most significant gaps and have them study the issue and come up with a plan. Present the plan to management. Execute. Being a best place to work attracts higher-level talent.

9. **Eliminate bureaucratic nonsense.** Many organizations have things that can get in the way of performance—lack of direction, inadequate resources and support, and poorly designed processes. These are all barriers to success. Start with direction. Does everyone know what they are expected to do and why? Do the mission, vision, and strategy translate to everyone's job? In your organization surveys, ask people if they know what they're expected to do. Address the gaps. Second, do people have the resources to do their jobs? Are budgets always tight? Are tools and supplies to do the job readily available? What about processes? Are they well designed? Apply practices such as TQM, Six Sigma, or business process engineering to make improvements. Study your policies and procedures. Are they user friendly? Do they require more time and attention than they need? Are there just enough steps to get the job done? Are the checks and balances the minimum needed to assure compliance? Ask employees to identify what gets in their way in surveys. Pay attention to streamlining organizational bureaucracy.

10. **Upgrade management.** If this area is a challenge for your organization, use the ten competencies listed above and apply them to managers. Select potential managers using this list of competencies. Use these competencies for performance evaluation and put them in the management 360°. Offer courses in these ten skills. Give feedback to managers on these ten skills. Put these ten skills in your morale and engagement surveys. Set people goals against these competencies. Use these competencies in succession management. Hire coaches who specialize in these ten skills.

SUGGESTED READINGS

Abramson, D. (2005). *Secrets of hiring top talent.* Round Hill, VA: Staff Dynamics.

Berger, L. A., & Berger, D. R. (2003). *The talent management handbook: Creating organizational excellence by identifying, developing, and promoting your best people.* New York, NY: McGraw-Hill.

Bradt, G., Check, J. A., & Pedraza, J. (2006). *The new leader's 100-day action plan.* Hoboken, NJ: John Wiley & Sons, Inc.

Brodie, J. M. (2006). Getting managers on board. *HR Magazine, 51*(11), 105-107.

Burkholder, N. C., Edwards, P. J., Sr., & Sartain, L. (Eds.). (2003). *On staffing.* New York, NY: John Wiley & Sons.

Chowdhury, S. (2001). *The talent era: Achieving a high return on talent.* Upper Saddle River, NJ: Financial Times Prentice Hall.

Ciampa, D., & Watkins, M. (1999). *Right from the start: Taking charge in a new leadership role.* Boston, MA: Harvard Business School Press.

Cohen, D. S. (2001). *The talent edge: A behavioral approach to hiring, developing, and keeping top performers.* Ontario, Canada: John Wiley & Sons Canada Limited.

Cohen, Y., & Pfeffer, J. (1986). Organizational hiring standards. *Administrative Science Quarterly, 31*, 1-24.

English, G. (2001). *Solving the people puzzle: Practical strategies for optimizing workforce performance.* Amherst, MA: HRD Press.

Honhson, L. K. (2005, June). Get your new managers moving. *Harvard Management Update, 10*(6), 3-5.

Jean, B. (1994). *Successful new employee orientation: Assess, plan, conduct, and evaluate your program* (2nd ed.). San Francisco, CA: Jossey-Bass/Pfeffer.

McCall, M. (1998). *High flyers: Developing the next generation of leaders.* Boston, MA: Harvard Business School Press.

Outlaw, W. (1998). *Smart staffing: How to hire, reward and keep top employees for your growing company.* Chicago, IL: Dearborn Publishing Group, Inc.

Sims, D. M. (2001). *Creative new employee orientation programs: Best practices, creative ideas, and activities for energizing your orientation program.* New York, NY: McGraw-Hill.

Smart, B. (2005). *Top grading: How leading companies win by hiring, coaching, and keeping the best people.* New York, NY: Penguin Group.

Tulgan, B. (2002). *Wining the talent wars: How to build a lean, flexible, high-performance workplace.* New York, NY: W. W. Norton & Company, Inc.

Watkins, M. (2003). *The first 90 days: Critical success strategies for new leaders at all levels*. Boston, MA: Harvard Business School Press.

Wick, C. (1996). *The learning edge*. New York, NY: McGraw-Hill.

Wick, C., Pollock, R., Jefferson, A., Flanagan, R., & Wilde, K. (2006). *The six disciplines of breakthrough learning: How to turn training and development into business results*. San Francisco, CA: Pfeffer.

CLUSTER I: ENGAGING EMPLOYEES

*When people can see which direction the leaders are going in
it becomes easier to motivate them.*
Lakshmi Mittal – Chairman and CEO,
Arcelor Mittal, world's largest steel company

Management is nothing more than motivating other people.
Lee Iacocca – Former Chairman, Chrysler Corporation

THE SIGNPOST

According to Woody Allen, "Eighty percent of success is showing up." That's a start, but you certainly want a lot more from your employees. You want them to be productive, to care about customers and other employees, to think, to be loyal to the organization, and to stay in your employment. In short, you want them engaged. Engaged employees will bring customers in and keep them coming back. They'll help themselves and, in the process, help the organization. Engaging employees is a key organization capability. Devote the attention, energy, and resources your engagement efforts deserve.

ITEMS

9. Have loyal and committed employees
29. Have strong trust between our top management and employees
49. Make employees feel like stakeholders
69. Measure and respond to employee engagement data

UNSKILLED

- Is unaware of or uninterested in the factors that engage employees
- Doesn't measure engagement and follow through to act on results
- Fails to hold managers accountable for engagement of their workgroups
- Tolerates bad bosses
- Doesn't communicate engagement results back to employees
- Doesn't develop engagement skills in managers
- Gives lip service to engagement but doesn't provide resources to make a difference
- Doesn't reward engagement
- Has managers that don't listen to employees
- Doesn't involve employees in improving engagement

SKILLED

- Understands the importance of engagement and the factors that impact it
- Demonstrates genuine commitment to increasing employee engagement
- Measures and monitors engagement on an ongoing basis
- Has managers fully committed to listening to and engaging employees
- Holds bosses responsible for engagement in their work units
- Acts on engagement results and involves employees where appropriate
- Separates chronic bad bosses from the organization
- Celebrates engagement progress and achievements
- Develops engagement skills in all managers
- Provides incentives and rewards to management for increasing employee engagement

SOME CAUSES

- Narcissistic top management
- Management is new and/or incompetent
- Employees not held in same regard as other stakeholders
- Poor internal communication
- Lack of compelling strategic focus
- Prevailing complacency and apathy
- Ill-defined corporate culture
- Lack of development and career opportunities
- Poor hiring practices
- Inappropriate organizational structure
- Imbalanced focus on results at all costs
- Extreme pressures from severe business conditions

THE TEN LEADERSHIP ARCHITECT® COMPETENCIES MOST ASSOCIATED WITH THIS CLUSTER (in order of connectedness)

33. Listening

27. Informing

18. Delegation

12. Conflict Management

36. Motivating Others

60. Building Effective Teams

65. Managing Vision and Purpose

41. Patience

19. Developing Direct Reports and Others

64. Understanding Others

THE MAP

Why engage? Why go through the effort? What's in it for the organization? Winning, that's what! Engagement buys you increased productivity. It buys you decreased turnover. It attracts better people to begin with. It's more fun. Engaged people take less sick days. Engaged people are more apt to cooperate and support change efforts. Engaged people bring their "A" game. Engaged employees pass along their enthusiasm to customers who buy more and stay longer. So it pays to engage. The principles of engagement are well known. There are endless surveys and studies about what tends to engage people. It's not easy. One of the primary engagement factors is the quality of the boss. How many good bosses have you had in your career? How many bad ones? Good bosses listen. They inform. They inspire. They delegate not only the task but the method and the appropriate level of authority as well. Good bosses bring out the best in people. They develop their people for the current job and the future as well. They build teams. Perhaps one-third or fewer of bosses are truly good bosses by those measures. Bad bosses cost organizations a lot in lost productivity and turnover. Organizations that engage their workforce are clear about the strategy, the mission, the vision. They set reasonable stretch goals. They reward high performance. They inform. They are supportive of risk and tolerant of the occasional well-intended mistake. They develop their employees and offer opportunities for full deployment of their skills. Most organizations are not engaging. Winning organizations are. It's not easy, but it's always worth the effort.

SOME REMEDIES

1. **Take a position on engagement.** Put a stake in the ground. Make engagement part of the organization's value statement and strategy. Create an engagement plan. Put the same effort and rigor into your engagement plan that you would for any other critical business function. If necessary, educate top management on the importance and the ROI of engagement. Set engagement goals. Apply engagement measures. Put engagement improvement goals into the incentives plans. Use improvement goals when evaluating managers. Require top managers to work the importance of engagement into their speeches. Create news about engagement and distribute it widely. Put it into the annual report. Create campaigns. Make engagement a major part of the strategic plan and cement it into the culture.

2. **Measure engagement.** Select a validated survey that provides normative data. Do not create your own survey. There are lots of good vendors out there. Pick one with norms and the capability to add a few of your own custom items. Measure engagement periodically, every two years at minimum. Annually is better. Have outside consultants review and report on the data. Pick consultants with lots of experience across both good and bad companies. Don't get fooled by

meta-grumbles. Every survey ever done has the item about "I'm paid well for what I do" at the bottom of the results. That's a meta-grumble. It may or may not mean you need to look at your pay system. That's why you need norms. If that item is at or above the norms, it probably isn't actionable. Same for "My opinions matter." "I am able to balance my work and personal lives." "I have been provided the training and development I need to advance my career." All of those types of items are at the bottom of every survey and are part of the anthropology of human organizations. Whether they are real problems or not depends upon how you compare to other organizations.

3. **Act on engagement results.** It's a best practice to measure engagement. It's a best practice to share the results with employees. It's a best practice to identify what's real. It's a worst practice to not act on what's real. It's a worst practice to not react at all. It's a worst practice to pretend you never asked the employees for their opinions. Many organizations survey; far fewer act on the survey. Many act on the wrong things. After separating what's real from the meta-grumbles, create an action plan. Involve as many people as possible. Form task groups to tackle specific issues. Assign a senior-level champion to each issue. Set goals and time frames. Communicate plans to employees. Track progress closely and frequently. Note every movement of the needle. Follow up. Act. Communicate progress. Communicate successes.

4. **Provide feedback to managers.** Although you want to measure engagement at the enterprise level, you also need to measure engagement at the workgroup level. Each workgroup has its own culture, driven mostly by the boss. Using the same survey results, look at engagement at the work unit level. Give the feedback first to the boss and then have the boss share it with the workgroup. If your organization has not done this before, someone from HR should facilitate the workgroup meetings. Each workgroup should have its own action plan against the results. Managers should be held accountable for acting on and improving their results.

5. **Provide training and development for managers.** Many, if not the majority of bosses, are not good at creating positive engagement. They need help. The good news is that the science and technology of engagement is well known. Bring in engagement experts. Buy a course. Offer an online engagement help service. Your engagement surveys can identify the managers who are having the most trouble. Get them the help they need. It doesn't have to be difficult. There are many techniques that are easy to learn and apply that make a real difference for employees. Teach them to your managers.

6. **Consider the value chain.** Track key business metrics of managers with high engagement and compare them to managers with low engagement. Follow the engagement out into the customer base. Make the economic case for the ROI on

your efforts for engagement. Track the cost of recruiting. Increases in engagement should cause people to want to work for the organization. Engagement should decrease hiring cost. It should increase retention. It should decrease sick days. It should reduce unexcused absences. Follow the metrics of engagement. It's a valuable feedback and reinforcement loop. Engagement should feed on itself.

7. **Embed engagement into HR systems.** If your organization is struggling with engagement, use the ten competencies listed above as a success profile for managers. If you have 360° feedback on managers, link it to their engagement scores. Identify the competencies that drive engagement and use them to create a success profile. Use that success profile for development, career discussions, promotions, and staffing decisions. Offer development opportunities and training on each competency. Engage skilled coaches to assist.

8. **Reward and celebrate engagement.** Provide tangible and intangible reinforcement to employees who demonstrate loyalty and commitment to the organization. Use it as a factor in pay decisions. Give people compensatory time off for completing tough assignments. Also offer other intangible, personalized reinforcements for deserving individuals. Those who are disengaged from the organization will realize that they aren't receiving the same benefits as others and will either change or leave the organization. For those who haven't gotten the message, a more direct intervention may be needed. Find examples of exemplary engagement and communicate them widely. Recognize improvements. Create awards for outstanding engagement achievements.

9. **Clean out the bad apples.** Bad bosses and bad employees take a big bite out of engagement. Not bad in the sense of lying, cheating, and stealing, but bad in the sense of unproductive attitude and not carrying their weight. The old saying that one bad apple can spoil the barrel is true about engagement. One employee who's lazy or has a bad attitude can impact many others. Identify the troublemakers. Give them candid, timely, and actionable feedback. Put them on a short improvement plan. Provide all of the help that is practical. Closely monitor progress or lack thereof. If there isn't a meaningful change, take decisive action. Do the same for managers. Festering bad attitudes grow.

10. **Dispel organizational myths.** Organizations own a distinct history. Identify that history and understand the stories that are told by employees to employees. Negative stories—those that have no constructive value—help perpetuate negative engagement. Counter the stories that are not true or are being negatively embellished. Give employees something positive to talk about. Inform employees. Don't keep them in the dark. Don't let them fill in information gaps with their own spin. Tell them the truth. Open the lines of communication upwards, downwards, and sideways.

DIMENSION IV: ATTRACTING/RETAINING/MOTIVATING TALENT

I: ENGAGING EMPLOYEES

SUGGESTED READINGS

Barrow, S., & Mosley, R., (2005). *The employer brand: Bringing the best of brand management to people at work* (2nd ed.). Chichester, England: John Wiley & Sons, Ltd.

Branham, L. (2001). *Keeping the people who keep you in business: 24 Ways to hang on to your most valuable talent*. New York, NY: AMACOM.

Branham, L. (2005). *The 7 Hidden reasons employees leave: How to recognize the subtle signs and act before it's too late*. New York, NY: AMACOM.

Ciancutti, A. R., & Steding, T. L. (2000). *Built on trust: Gaining competitive advantage in any organization*. Lincolnwood, IL: NTC/Contemporary Publishing Group, Inc.

Drake, S., Gulman, M. J., & Roberts, S. (2005). *Light their fire: Using internal marketing to ignite employee performance and wow your customers*. Chicago, IL: Kaplan Business.

Frank, F. D., Finnegan, R. P., & Taylor, C. R. (2004). The race for talent: Retaining and engaging workers in the 21st century. *Human Resource Planning*, *27*(3), 12-25.

Huselid, M. A., Becker, B. E., & Beatty, R .W. (2005). *The workforce scorecard: Managing human capital to execute strategy*. Boston, MA: Harvard Business School Press.

Sartain, L., & Schumann, M. (2006). *Brand from the inside: Eight essentials to emotionally connect your employees to your business*. San Francisco, CA: Jossey-Bass.

Seijts, G. H., & Crim, D. (2006). What engages employees the most or, the ten Cs of employee engagement. *Ivey Business Journal*, *70*(4), 1-5.

Towers Perrin Talent Report. (2003). *Working today: Understanding what drives employee engagement*. Retrieved January 11, 2007 from http://www.towersperrin.com/tp/jsp/search.jsp

Ulrich, D., & Brockbank, W. (2005). *The HR value proposition*. Boston, MA: Harvard Business School Press.

Whitener, E. M., Brodt, S. E., Korsgaard, M. A., & Werner, J. M. (1998). Managers as initiators of trust: An exchange relationship for understanding managerial trustworthy behavior. *Academy of Management Review*, *23*, 513-530.

CLUSTER J: ACCOUNTABILITY AND REWARDS

There are two things people want more than sex and money –
recognition and praise.
Mary Kay Ash – Founder, Mary Kay Cosmetics

Executives owe it to the organization and to their fellow workers
not to tolerate nonperforming individuals in important jobs.
Peter Drucker – Business theorist, author, and strategist

THE SIGNPOST
Organizational performance is driven by individuals working together. Lackluster individual performance means subpar organizational performance. Organizations must address the performance of individuals by providing opportunities for purposeful work, setting clear goals, measuring accomplishments, and providing meaningful consequences.

ITEMS
10. Translate individual and collective goals and objectives into performance standards
30. Lay out clear accountabilities and consequences for everyone in the organization
50. Use compensation as a tool to focus and drive performance
70. Have a significant amount of pay at risk for top management
86. Reward people differentially based upon their overall contribution to the organization
92. Concentrate on measuring results with a balanced measures scorecard

UNSKILLED
- Fails to create alignment between business goals and rewards
- Uses inappropriate mix of base pay and variable compensation
- Doesn't create a high-performance culture
- Fails to clearly set expectations and communicate goals
- Doesn't fully understand or utilize intangible rewards
- Manages through antecedents and bribery rather than consequences
- Doesn't use appropriate timing in delivering reinforcement
- Focuses on minimum performance rather than optimum
- Fails to personalize recognition
- Relies on one type of incentive to provide motivation
- Fails to differentiate performance and merit pay; rates most employees high
- Rewards management, even when overall business performance misses targets

SKILLED

- Clearly defines the link between performance and rewards
- Uses a comprehensive approach to motivation using a variety of incentives
- Effectively celebrates accomplishments with employees
- Recognizes and reinforces incremental improvements in performance
- Knows employees and shapes reinforcement so it's personalized and meaningful
- Explains how individual performance impacts the team and the organization
- Is willing to change approaches to compensation in response to business conditions
- Embraces conversation; talks candidly about performance, whether it's poor or outstanding
- Has courage to discriminate, to reward high performers at the expense of low performers
- Is able to remove emotion and subjectivity from performance assessment
- Clearly communicates expectations and performance goals
- Establishes effective measures of behavior and of accomplishments
- Fosters loyalty through openness and demonstrating trust
- Puts part of compensation at risk to be determined by performance

SOME CAUSES

- Lack of managerial courage
- Complacency
- Tolerance for mediocrity
- Poor internal communication
- Conflict avoidance
- Lack of business acumen
- Intolerant of diversity
- Unsophisticated talent management practices
- Failure to discriminate performance levels and treat people differently
- Unwillingness to consider new approaches to compensation
- Us vs. them (management vs. employees) mentality

THE TEN LEADERSHIP ARCHITECT® COMPETENCIES MOST ASSOCIATED WITH THIS CLUSTER (in order of connectedness)

35. Managing and Measuring Work

56. Sizing Up People

53. Drive for Results

13. Confronting Direct Reports

50. Priority Setting

20. Directing Others

47. Planning

5. Business Acumen

12. Conflict Management

27. Informing

THE MAP

Why is management so difficult? Managers can excel at basic managerial tasks such as planning, organizing, and controlling, yet still fall short of succeeding at what business author Mary Parker Follett described nearly a century ago as "the art of getting things done through others." It's that fourth basic managerial function—motivation—that often proves so elusive. Why? Haven't we all read Maslow, McGregor, Herzberg, others? There's no shortage of theory on motivation, yet most managers still don't get it—they don't understand the paradox—we're all the same and we're all different. Basically, you, me, and those we work with all need to get along with the people with whom we work, believe we're being paid fairly for our contribution, and leave work each day feeling some sense of pride in what we've accomplished. Those three things are pretty universal. Yet the personalization of those three elements, the way they're filtered through each individual's value system, complicates things for managers. We're all the same and all different. We all have different hot buttons and reasons for doing what we do. Effective managers understand that. They satisfy those universal needs but do so in a way that is personalized for their people. Organizations that create high-performance cultures empower their managers to provide meaningful consequences and help them do so. In those organizations, management is largely about managing consequences because only positive and certain consequences sustain performance over the long haul. Those high-performance cultures don't give a thought about minimum performance. They don't tolerate it. The focus is all about optimum performance, about becoming faster, better, leaner, more profitable every day, every quarter, every year. The business strategy is clearly communicated and rewards are structured to reinforce that strategy. Strategy is translated into goals and measures. Everyone knows what to do, how to do it, and what to expect in return. Simply put, talented people work best when they have a set of goals and measures and predictable rewards for success. In the best organizations there is an openness and directness not found in less-successful organizations. There is pride, loyalty, trust, and a sense of ownership that is fostered by the effective reward strategy that mixes tangible and intangible reinforcement as a consequence for frequent incremental improvements, not just for recognition of annual accomplishments. Celebration is in the air because the team is winning. Now there's the place to work!

SOME REMEDIES

1. **Align the rewards strategy with the business strategy.** This is Business 101. What outcomes do you want? What's required of employees to achieve those

65

outcomes? How will you measure it? People pay attention to what gets measured and, in the long run, will put in sustained effort for what gets rewarded. If you want to increase customer satisfaction, don't provide incentives to customer service reps based on the number of calls per hour they handle, for instance. Their natural response will be to shortchange service in order to pump up their productivity. It's necessary to have a multipronged incentive strategy to reward a mix of behaviors and avoid sacrificing one or more of the Fundamental Four: quality, productivity, timeliness, and cost. Of course, if your business strategy changes, it follows then that your rewards strategy must change to support it. When you've got it right, everyone wins.

2. **Make the link between performance and reward crystal clear.** Most organizations have merit pay systems. Most don't work for two primary reasons: (1) Employees don't understand the system because it's mysterious at best or secretive at worst; and (2) Organizations don't do what they say they're going to do. If you're going to make 50% of merit bonuses dependent on organizational performance measured by a combination of factors that include return on assets, net new business growth, and customer loyalty, you'd better make sure employees understand how those things are measured and how they individually impact those measures. If you proclaim a desire to reward top performance by awarding 30% of the merit budget pool to the top 10% of performers and withhold all merit pay from the bottom 10% of performers, you better have managers with the courage to follow through and execute that plan. Tell employees how they will be rewarded, make sure they understand how to earn the bonus, and then pay it out like you said you would.

3. **Set appropriate goals.** Generally, people perform best with achievable stretch goals—goals that can realistically be reached by standing tall and putting forth significant effort. Goals set too high or too low demotivate. Goals that are too high are seen as unreasonable, so why bother? Goals that are too low leave people coasting. This a balancing act complicated by the need to set stretch goals for individuals as well as business units. Give this adequate attention and have performers collaborate. Often an individual performer will set the bar higher than management dares, and the sense of ownership created by the collaboration will lead to greater achievement. Build in interim progress goals to break down stretch goals into more manageable chunks and to facilitate frequent assessment, dialog, feedback, and coaching.

4. **Use a mix of tangible and intangible reinforcement.** Tangible can be touched. Cash is top on that list, but far from the only thing. Non-cash tangible reinforcement should be your first consideration for providing "spot bonuses" to recognize extraordinary effort and accomplishment. The reward can range from simple—a pair of movie tickets—to extravagant—an all-expenses-paid weekend

in Manhattan with theatre tickets and fine dining. Non-cash tangible rewards can leverage your rewards budget; movie tickets costing $16 will be remembered by the employee far longer than a $20 bill. Such things build employee loyalty. Never underestimate the impact of tangible reinforcement, but never, ever neglect the power of intangible reinforcement. Intangible reinforcement is the manager's best tool for motivating employees on a day-to-day basis because it's free and it's effective. Pats on the back, words of praise, and don't forget handwritten notes—all have incredible meaning to employees. To do them right, make sure they're genuine—the manager believes the message; they're legitimate—they actually follow good performance; and they're meaningful—they are delivered in a context and format that the employee values.

5. **Use the right mix of financial rewards.** Intangible rewards can't do it all. Employees need financial compensation, and when they complain about pay, understand that their real concern most likely really is about their pay (not about their boss, working conditions, or something else). In addition to base salary, you have many options for providing variable compensation: spot bonuses, merit bonuses, gain sharing, profit sharing, equity, and others. Get a handle on how to best utilize all the elements of compensation by studying compensation resources listed in the references. Variable compensation gives you considerable flexibility and tremendous power in creating a high-performance culture. Use base pay to provide a market-based primary reward for employees' sustained contributions to the organization. Focus the employee's performance on vital measures of success with variable compensation components. They will enable you to be responsive and flexible in rewarding results.

6. **Be timely.** Positive reinforcement should occur every day for every employee. Reinforcement. Not bribery. Reinforcement is a positive consequence that follows something done well. Bribery precedes desired behavior—and it's not effective. So managers need to be on the lookout for the right behaviors, incremental performance improvements, and small accomplishments. When seen, those opportunities should be pounced on! Employees should know that management is paying attention. They should be told their accomplishments are noticed and appreciated. Is that so difficult? If you fail to do this, you're failing as an organization.

7. **Make it personal.** Remember the paradox? We all require certain rewards from our jobs, the universal motivators. But we are all individuals and have different value systems. Some employees will be ecstatic when you reward them with a half-day off as a reward for long hours they put in over the past week to meet a critical business objective. Other employees wouldn't respond so positively. Do you know what motivates your employees? If not, ask. Understand what turns them on. Don't inadvertently punish a self-conscious introverted employee

DIMENSION IV: ATTRACTING/RETAINING/MOTIVATING TALENT

J: ACCOUNTABILITY

by praising her in public when she'd rather have a discreet, private show of appreciation. Don't deny your self-assured hotshot the public recognition he craves by delivering your praise in private. It's simple. Just know your employees and treat them like they want to be treated. Empower your managers to treat people as individuals. Make sure your policies and procedures allow some flex to accommodate as many individuals as possible.

8. **Become an open book.** Compensation is a sensitive subject, and making compensation public is considered taboo in most work cultures. There is research evidence that secrecy creates more troubles than does openness. In a vacuum, employees can make all kinds of assumptions that lead to perceived inequities. Better that pay scales—at least the ranges for pay grades—are clearly communicated and there is no secret about employee grades. This becomes even more important at higher pay grades. Threatened? Why? At least give this serious thought. Openness will foster trust, not suspicion. While you're at it, consider how you can provide more information for employees about the organization's performance. Opening your books to the extent possible engenders a sense of ownership, loyalty, trust, and helps employees see ways they contribute to the organization's success. Openness is a hallmark of high-performance cultures.

9. **Celebrate incremental successes.** Winners celebrate. Major victories. Small improvements. Anything positive is an opportunity for celebration. Use a combination of formal, planned celebrations, like awards banquets, to simple, unplanned hallway gatherings to recognize the two employees who just team-tagged a response to a customer-service problem and saved an important customer. Learn how to celebrate. Coffee and bagels. Pizza. Little things go a long way. Invite the right people. Select the right people to provide the recognition. Incorporate the right symbolism. Make it genuine. Make sure it's deserved, that it's about real success. And have fun with it!

10. **Model the behaviors you want in others.** Leadership 101. Walk the talk. It all starts with your leaders. The standards to which leaders hold themselves must be above the standards to which others are held. If not, be assured that employees will see right through the sham and disdain the rewards structure. If the organization is targeting quality, executives should set the quality standard with their work. If the organization is targeting productivity, executives should be working rings around everyone else. Top management should quietly and confidently do the job that raises the bar for everyone in the organization.

SUGGESTED READINGS

Chingos, P. T. (2002). *Paying for performance: A guide to compensation management* (2nd ed.). New York: John Wiley & Sons, Inc.

Connellan, T. K. (2003). *Bring out the best in others! Three keys for business leaders, educators, coaches and parents.* Austin, TX: Bard Press.

Daniels. A. C. (2000). *Bringing out the best in people: How to apply the astonishing power of positive reinforcement.* New York, NY: McGraw-Hill, Inc.

Fournies, F. F. (1999). *Coaching for improved work performance.* New York, NY: McGraw-Hill.

Gostick, A., & Elton, C. (2001). *Managing with carrots: Using recognition to attract and retain the best people.* Layton, UT: Gibbs Smith, Publisher.

Hale, R. L., & Maehling, R. F. (1992). *Recognition redefined: Building self-esteem at work.* Minneapolis, MN: Tennant Company.

Kouzes, J. M., & Posner, B. Z. (2002). *The leadership challenge.* San Francisco, CA: John Wiley & Sons, Inc.

Kouzes, J. M., & Posner, B. Z. (2003). *Encouraging the heart: A leader's guide to reward and recognizing others.* San Francisco, CA: Jossey-Bass.

Lawler, E. E. (1981). Merit pay: Fact or fiction? *Management Review, 70*(4), 50-53.

Lawler, E., III, & Lawler, E. E. (2003). *Treat people right: How organizations and employees can create a win/win relationship to achieve high performance at all levels.* San Francisco, CA: Jossey-Bass.

Luthans, F., & Stajkovic, A. D. (1999). Reinforce for performance: The need to go beyond pay and even rewards. *Academy of Management Executive, 13,* 49-57.

Nelson, B. (1994). *1001 Ways to reward employees.* New York, NY: Workman Publishing Company, Inc.

Rampersad, H. K. (2003). *Total performance scorecard: Redefining management to achieve performance with integrity.* Burlington, MA: Butterworth-Heinemann.

Stack, J., & Burlingham, B. (1994). *The great game of business.* New York, NY: Currency.

Stajkovic, A. D., & Luthans, F. (1997). A meta-analysis of the effects of organization behavior modification on task performance, 1975-95. *Academy of Management Journal, 40,* 1122-1149.

Ulrich, D., Zenger, J., & Smallwood, N. (1999). *Results-based leadership.* Boston, MA: Harvard Business School Press.

Wiley, C. (1997). What motivates employees according to over 40 years of motivation survey. *International Journal of Manpower, 18*, 263-280.

Zingheim, P. K., & Schuster, J. R. (2000). *Pay people right: Breakthrough reward strategies to create great companies*. San Francisco, CA: Jossey-Bass Publishers.

CLUSTER K: LEVERAGING CULTURE

Example is not the main thing in influencing others, it's the only thing.
Albert Schweitzer – Theologian, philosopher, and physician

*Take good care of your employees and they'll take good care of your customers,
and the customers will come back.*
J. Willard Marriott – Founder, Marriott International

THE SIGNPOST
Culture can be thought of as the sum of the habits of the individuals in the organization. It's the way we do things and think about things, a reflection of our collective attitudes, beliefs, and values. Culture shapes how decisions are made, how fast the organization moves, how it takes risks, and how it develops talent. Culture affects employee engagement, recruitment, and retention. It directly impacts the organization's performance.

ITEMS
11. Use corporate culture as a tool for linking with key customers and strategy
31. Adapt our culture to the brand or identification of the firm in the mind of the customer
51. Translate the desired culture into a set of employee behaviors and practices
71. Model our core values and culture

UNSKILLED
- Fails to passionately create a clear vision about what the organization is all about
- Doesn't clearly articulate the values to which the organization adheres
- Fails to create alignment between the culture and the business strategy
- Informs inadequately or with mixed messages about strategy and culture
- Can't explain the link between the vision and values and aligned behaviors
- Doesn't understand or appreciate the link between internal and external branding
- Fails to walk the talk; executive behavior doesn't match messages
- Misaligns organizational structure with stated cultural goals
- Creates policies and procedures that are counter to cultural goals
- Underestimates the importance of the customer's perception of culture
- Does not create a strong cultural brand visible to customers and other stakeholders
- Undervalues the informal organization; relies primarily on formal policies and procedures

71

SKILLED

- Clearly and passionately communicates the vision and values of the organization
- Enthusiastically works to purposefully align culture to the strategy
- Lives and breathes the values
- Never misses an opportunity to reinforce the culture through communication
- Pays attention to the internal brand; creates a branding strategy around culture
- Uses storytelling to convey cultural messages in a way that has impact
- Makes sure that policies and procedures reinforce the goals of the culture
- Effectively uses everyday, informal behaviors to reinforce the culture
- Reinforces and rewards aligned behavior in others
- Designs organizational structures to enhance and reinforce the culture
- Considers cultural fit in all hiring and staffing decisions
- Promotes the culture externally, strengthening the company image in the customer's mind

SOME CAUSES

- Undeveloped business strategy
- Unclear about vision and values
- Misalignment between strategy and culture
- Poor internal communication
- Narrow perspective
- Complacency; doesn't consider culture important
- Too action and results oriented to reflect
- Difficulty with complexity
- Too fragmented to form a cohesive culture
- Can't keep up with disruptive change

THE TEN LEADERSHIP ARCHITECT® COMPETENCIES MOST ASSOCIATED WITH THIS CLUSTER (in order of connectedness)

65. Managing Vision and Purpose

51. Problem Solving

52. Process Management

2. Dealing with Ambiguity

15. Customer Focus

27. Informing

38. Organizational Agility

46. Perspective

64. Understanding Others

36. Motivating Others

THE MAP

Culture is the "invisible" part of how organizations operate. It plays out in the ways people think and how they behave at work. Culture is the collective sum of the habits of the individuals in the organization. These habits are guided by shared attitudes, beliefs, and values that determine how and why people make decisions and choose to act, particularly under stress and lack of direct guidance. You can tell a lot about culture by looking at the discretionary factors that reinforce it—manners of speech, dress, facilities, symbols, rituals and ceremonies, etc. Even if it's not explicitly expressed in words, culture is real and present and denoted by what people actually do. Culture complements and is reinforced by formal organization elements—strategy, organizational structures, policies, and procedures. A strong and aligned culture is a significant enabler of strategy execution. A well-defined culture can enhance the organization's reputation and brand in the marketplace in the eyes of customers and investors. It is essential to manage the culture in a way that mirrors the attributes for which the firm wants to be recognized. This branding effort is a powerful tool in terms of strengthening a company's standing, and leaders of successful companies are adept at creating this linkage. The more a culture is aligned with the strategy, tactics, and needs of the customer, the more effective the organization will be. A strong culture allows people more freedom because it will guide them in their decision making and actions without having to be told what to do by managers.

SOME REMEDIES

1. **Align your culture.** Armed with your organization's strategy and value statements, define what the aligned culture should be. What do you care about? What do you believe about the business? About your customers? About employees? What do you want to achieve? What behaviors do you want to promote to achieve your goals? The culture that promotes those behaviors is an aligned and effective culture. It will shape how all stakeholders—customers, employees, investors—and the rest of the world perceive the organization. Once you have determined what the culture should be, do a culture audit and see what it is. Find the gaps and close them. As an example, if your strategy and values point to speed, consider how your culture promotes that characteristic. How do you talk about speed? How do you reward it? How do you celebrate it? How are decisions made? How do policies and procedures impact speed of decision making? What about the organization structure? Anything and everything that impacts behaviors related to speed should be considered and addressed. Changing values and beliefs can be a long and arduous process. Changing policies and processes is easier, and that's exactly where to begin to work on values and beliefs. Make changes in your communication, your policies, your practices—make changes in everything that's observable to bring them into alignment with the values and vision you want to

promote. It will take some time, but the beliefs and values will eventually follow, and you'll have created a strong aligned culture that best serves the strategic vision.

2. **Understand how customers see your brand.** Conduct surveys, focus groups, interviews, and other market research with your best customers and investors. Figure out what your company is actually known for and what your current and prospective customers want you to be known for. Look at your company's book value versus market value for an indication of how investors regard the intangible value of your brand. Seek to comprehend all the factors that contribute to these perceptions, including your products, your marketing, your message, your customer service, your reputation, comparison to the competition, etc. Measure these both quantitatively and qualitatively. Determine the extent to which key customer views align with your vision. Find the gaps and close them.

3. **Understand how your employees see your brand.** Conduct an internal cultural survey. Ask employees how they see the external brand and assess the internal culture. To get a measure of alignment, ask employees to identify which attributes and behaviors would represent the way customers prefer to see you, and then determine the extent to which these are reflected in the culture. Identify and explore the gaps to determine the highest priority ones to address.

4. **Engage employees in the alignment challenge.** Inform employees about the results of the internal and external surveys and the implications of the gaps. Engage them in determining how to address any gaps. Use all methods of communication, including face-to-face, team, department, location-specific, and organization-wide meetings. Keep reiterating by formal presentations, memos, video conferencing, satellite broadcasts, podcasts, phone, voicemail, and email. Assign a manager to each gap and create work groups and task forces to come up with suggestions and action plans to close the gaps.

5. **Translate strategy and culture into behaviors and competencies.** Determine what behaviors and competencies best reflect the strategy and culture. Translate the strategy and culture into the specific behaviors that people need to demonstrate in order to achieve the strategic and cultural objectives. Ensure that these are built into performance expectations along with objectives, technical competencies, and job-related behavioral competencies. Measure your leaders with 360° assessments on the key competencies and behaviors and insist that they work on any areas that would improve their alignment. See that development plans include ways of enhancing these areas and that progress against the plans is measured. Hold managers accountable to walk the strategic and cultural talk.

6. **Involve everyone.** Engage people up front in prioritizing cultural needs based on gaps between the vision and the reality. Ask them to help figure out how best to address the shortcomings. Bring together groups of employees holding various

perspectives on any issue to be addressed. Lead them in establishing a shared vision, identifying related problems and obstacles, prioritizing them, and then immediately going after the low-hanging fruit. Ask them to create action plans to address all of the other issues that include specific steps, responsible parties, target dates, and follow-up strategies.

7. **Communicate consistently and persistently.** Congruence is important. Involve every manager in a coordinated effort to articulate the key messages. Develop processes to systematically convey the branding concepts throughout the organization. Periodically ask people at different levels and in various segments of the business to describe the company's culture, their degree of alignment with that culture, and what you should work on to better connect the culture to your brand.

8. **Maintain a customer focus.** While enhancing your culture and addressing internal organizational workings and politics, it's easy to lose sight of the customer. Don't. Rather, involve the customer in building your culture. Invite customers in frequently to tell their stories and report on brand alignment. Ensure that your metrics are not based prevalently on inward-facing activities. There should be considerable focus on customer-facing accomplishments. Seamlessly connect the internal and external brands. Use the aligned internal culture as a marketing tool. Consider how marketing communication and advertising can reflect the power of your aligned internal culture and brand. Present your cultural norms in recruiting and employee brochures to attract talent that will fit.

9. **Engage employees by storytelling.** Use stories to build alignment and provide examples of connections between the external brand image and internal culture. Weave engaging narratives and use anecdotes reflecting the customer perspective to capture the hearts of people and effectively influence their behavior. Have people share their own stories, so that their voices, as well as those of customers, are reflected in the culture. Keep linking back to the way in which aligning with the culture and brand will benefit them.

10. **Walk the talk.** Use the power of modeling. Leaders drive the creation and management of culture. They must take ownership of culture, live it, breathe it. Employees are always watching. They listen to what leaders say, but more importantly, they watch what leaders do. Your leaders should consciously strive to make their actions and words positive, client-focused, and aligned with the values. Be transparent about the way in which your decisions support the brand. Keep taking stock of how you are doing in this regard, and figure out how you can be even clearer in your modeling. Don't give people an excuse to act in a way that is not aligned with the envisioned culture. Hold your leaders accountable.

SUGGESTED READINGS

Barrett, R. (2006). *Building a values-driven organization: A whole systems approach to cultural transformation*. Burlington, MA: Butterworth-Heinemann.

Bridges, W. (2003). *Managing transitions, making the most of change* (2nd ed.). Cambridge, MA: Perseus Books Group.

Davis, S. M. (1984). *Managing corporate culture*. Cambridge, MA: Ballinger Publishing Co.

Deal, T. E., & Kennedy, A. A. (2000). *Corporate cultures*. New York, NY: Perseus Books Group.

Gallagher, R. (2002). *The soul of an organization: Understanding the values that drive successful corporate cultures*. Chicago, IL: Kaplan Business.

Katzenbach, J. R. (2000). *Peak performance: Aligning the hearts and minds of your employees*. Boston, MA: Harvard Business School Press.

Kotter, J. P. (1992). *Corporate culture and performance*. New York, NY: Free Press.

Kouses, J. M., & Posner, B. Z. (2006). *A leader's legacy*. New York, NY: Jossey-Bass.

Nadler, D. A. (1997). *Champions of change: How CEOs and their companies are mastering the skills of radical change*. San Francisco, CA: Jossey Bass.

Pohlman, R. A., Gardiner, G. S., & Heffes, E. M. (2000). *Value driven management: How to create and maximize value over time for organizational success*. New York, NY: AMACOM.

Schein, E. H. (2004). *Organizational culture and leadership* (3rd ed.). New York, NY: Jossey-Bass.

Ulrich, D., & Smallwood, N. (2006). Leadership as brand. In F. Hesselbein and M. Goldsmith (Eds.), *The leader of the future 2: Visions, strategies, and practices for the new era*. San Francisco, CA: Jossey Bass.

CLUSTER L: MANAGING COMMUNICATION

For me, words are a form of action, capable of influencing change.
Ingrid Bengis – Feminist writer and novelist

Self-expression must pass into communication for its fulfillment.
Pearl Buck – Writer and Nobel Prize winner

THE SIGNPOST

Communication powerfully impacts organizational alignment and performance. The frequency of communication, the volume, channels, content, the openness of communication—all these things impact the organization's ability to learn and to change. Communication impacts employee attitudes and engagement. It influences customers to embrace your brand. It's hard to imagine an aspect of organizational performance not affected by communication.

ITEMS

12. Create a shared mind-set at all levels and in all employees to focus their efforts
32. Keep communications focused on the right messages
52. Use multiple and innovative methods to share information
72. Have an effective communication process in place for keeping our employees informed on important issues

UNSKILLED

- Sends mixed messages
- Holds information close to the vest
- Relies on one-way communication
- Fails to listen to understand or learn
- Rejects feedback and criticism
- Overwhelms with irrelevant information; doesn't focus on key messages
- Doesn't customize the message to the audience
- Fails to use a variety of channels and methods
- Doesn't achieve clarity; messages are disorganized or ambiguous
- Doesn't listen for feedback or understanding
- Alienates some audiences with insensitive or inappropriate messages
- Fails to deliver communication in a timely manner

SKILLED

- Considers audience and purpose before crafting the message
- Consistently incorporates values and strategy in communication
- Frequently checks for understanding and adjusts message as required
- Uses a variety of channels, people, and media technologies to share information
- Embraces honest, direct feedback from all sources and acts on it
- Aims for clarity of purpose and straightforward, candid messages
- Purposely overcommunicates on issues of strategic importance
- Thoroughly communicates in advance of pending change
- Increases communications during crises and periods of change
- Demonstrates openness and truthfulness in communication
- Considers timeliness and volume of messages to achieve optimum effect
- Provides context with the message to assist with understanding

SOME CAUSES

- Lack of trust
- Lack of strategic clarity
- Fear of loss of control or power
- Aloof, inaccessible management
- Failure to listen
- Unorganized
- Organizational barriers, silos
- Leader defensiveness
- Gatekeeper mentality regarding information
- Inadequate communication systems and technology
- Insensitive to audience needs
- Belief that information is proprietary

THE TEN LEADERSHIP ARCHITECT® COMPETENCIES MOST ASSOCIATED WITH THIS CLUSTER (in order of connectedness)

27. Informing
64. Understanding Others
65. Managing Vision and Purpose
36. Motivating Others
47. Planning
52. Process Management
46. Perspective
49. Presentation Skills
51. Problem Solving
33. Listening

THE MAP

A disruption in information flow will hurt an organization even faster than a disruption in the availability of capital or raw materials. Without timely and accurate information, we can't effectively make decisions or take actions with any assurance. Of course, organizations create information as well as use it. But simply taking the time and being willing to share critical information is only half the battle. Organizations that effectively manage communication use a variety of approaches, a variety of media, a variety of channels. They use meetings, newsletters, bulletin boards, Web sites, videos, supervisors, executive leaders, and other methods to distribute timely and relevant information. It's important to provide clear messages about what we're supposed to be doing, how we're doing, how the competition is faring, how technology is changing, changes in the larger environment, how we're adapting, and more. Messages might include quarterly financial reports, board of director feedback, or responses to media commentary. Keeping employees informed of organization-relevant information helps develop increased ownership, buy-in, engagement, and commitment to the organization and its goals. Keeping the messages relevant allows a greater volume of targeted messages to be sent because workers are not overloaded with irrelevant information. Communicate frequently to ensure employees know what the organization is doing and why at all times. Reinforce the guiding principles found in your mission, strategy, and value statements frequently. These are keys to driving organizational decisions and almost impossible to overcommunicate. Employees kept in the loop feel valued and are more likely to work toward helping reach collective goals. Don't neglect to provide timely announcements about all organization issues of interest to employees—personnel changes, promotions, resignations, awards, team celebrations, etc. These are easily overlooked but, when forgotten, strike a blow against employee engagement. Employees shouldn't be surprised by company decisions and actions. Employees with a common mind-set based upon timely and accurate information will act in concert with greater efficiency and effectiveness.

SOME REMEDIES

1. **Communicate to drive business strategy.** Employee communication is not optional for effective organizations. You are encouraging participation and feedback from employees in part because it helps build morale, buy-in, commitment, and involvement around the business strategy. Involved and engaged employees are more productive. They know what the organizational goals are and how they're expected to contribute. Informed employees are easier to retain. Absenteeism and turnover decrease when employees are adequately informed. Additionally, engaged employees more easily gain access to new markets. They're more likely to contribute ideas and will more aggressively drive improvements in product and service. Engaged employees seek competitive-edge customer information and act on it. When everyone is on the same page in the

playbook, there is less friction, more efficiency. Embrace focused and timely internal communication as part of the strategy.

2. **Craft the message with care.** Treat employee communication like an ad campaign. Craft the message by carefully considering the audience and purpose. What important information do employees need to do their jobs effectively? Engage an internal or external PR staff member to help create key messages. Establish context around the message. How was the strategy created? Where did the values come from? What's the competition doing? How will you respond? How will accomplishments be measured? How were objectives and goals set? Who is accountable for what? What are the rewards and consequences for excellent performance? Where are the resources? What is the best way to get things done? Who can I ask for help? A second category of communications is what employees would like to know. This is information that's not essential for getting the job done, but it helps employees feel involved and in the know. Don't ignore it.

3. **Use multiple methods to communicate.** Everyone is busy and on the go. People can be hard to reach. Use as many media and channels as practical to communicate. Employ new communication technologies effectively. Create an employee Web site. Videos. Special forums for information sharing. Information lunches. Newsletters. Build internal communication channels. Whether through a company-wide email distribution list or a more traditional publication, make sure employees find out about major happenings from someone within the organization rather than public media sources. Technology can sometimes be a barrier. If the internet/intranet is used to communicate, make sure everyone has access. Shared on-site kiosks may be needed for employees who don't have computer access from their desk or workstation. Supervisors sometimes block the flow of top-down information—they need to be trained in the benefits of information-sharing, but must also be willing to allow reasonable on-site access to technology.

4. **Use solid principles of communication:**

   - **Two-way communication.** Do not simply provide one-way messages— listen to employees as well. Check for understanding. Solicit information from all employees. Make it an information exchange.

   - **Solicit questions from hesitant employees.** Many questions are left unanswered, not because an answer doesn't exist, but because no one asked the question. If employees are reluctant to speak up in one-on- one or small group information-sharing sessions, administer anonymous employee opinion surveys. Ask how consumers are reacting to the organization's products and messages. Ask if the company's mission and principles are clear and understood. Ask if employees feel they are receiving enough information about their employer. Adapt, follow up, and monitor progress.

- **Involve the customer.** Create a process to get pertinent and relevant customer information into the flow through surveys, focus groups, site visits, etc.

- **Consider the audience.** Enterprise-wide communication requires special consideration to ensure the message is clear to all. It's important to consider reading and comprehension levels and native languages. Adjust the communication to meet varied needs in the audience.

- **Stay focused.** There is a time and a place for birthday, anniversary, and softball team announcements. Keep these bits of information separated from organization-relevant messages.

5. **Make key decision makers more visible.** Web sites can help. Summaries of executive speeches or short biographies help keep people informed and break down perceptions that hierarchies present information-sharing barriers. Executives who can be seen and heard are more likely to be trusted. Get as many executives up and in front of groups of people as frequently as possible.

6. **Manage information.** Create systems to collect and analyze incoming information. In most organizations, people and units have useful information that is hard to access or poorly organized. There needs to be a centralized capacity to take in information and judge its usefulness. Customer data. Competitor data. Consumer trends. Quality feedback. Process gaps. Procedures. Job aids. Relevant research and articles. Create a way to assemble these bits of information that all employees know about and have access to. An internal Web site with various categories for entering information works well.

7. **Keep communication metrics.** Decide how to measure the effectiveness of your communication system and efforts. Look to both process and outcome measures. How will you know if the information is getting out and has had the intended effect? Use evaluations to provide feedback for message-makers and deliverers.

8. **Involve employees.** Employees want to contribute in a meaningful way. Increasing employee involvement does not mean that every employee needs a voice in decision making. Simply being honest and open with information is one way to make employees feel involved without directly including them in specific decision-making processes. Connect your engagement survey metrics to your communication metrics. Learn what messages and methods are most effective in moving the needle on employee engagement.

9. **Engender trust.** Communicate bad news quickly and forthrightly. Anticipate crises and have communication prepared in advance. Come clean when something goes wrong, when a commitment isn't kept, when something is done to violate the organization's values. Openness and honesty and quick responses should be the norm.

10. **Act.** Communication is more than sharing information about what's occurred and why. It's also the expression of intent. Follow through and act on feedback. Follow through and act on your communication metrics. Do what you say you're going to do. If you don't, people will soon tune you out. Communication that is not backed up by action will fall on deaf ears.

SUGGESTED READINGS

Argenti, P. A. (1998). Strategic employee communications. *Human Resource Management, 37*, 199-206.

Argenti, P. A., & Forman, J. (2002). *The power of corporate communication: Crafting the voice and image of your business*. New York, NY: McGraw-Hill.

Brandon, M. (1997). From the three Bs to the high Cs: History of employee communication. *Communication World, 14*(5/6), 18-21.

Gray, R., & Robertson, L. (2005). Effective internal communication starts at the top. *Communication World, 22*(4), 26-28.

Herington, C., Scott, D., & Johnson, L. W. (2005). Focus group exploration of firm-employee relationship strength. *Qualitative Market Research: An International Journal, 8*, 256-276.

Holtz, S. (2003). *Corporate conversations: A guide to crafting effective and appropriate internal communications*. New York, NY: AMACOM.

Ng, T. W. H., Butts, M. M., Vandenberg, R. J., DeJoy, D. M., & Wilson, M. G. (2006). Effects of management communication, opportunity for learning, and work schedule flexibility on organizational commitment. *Journal of Vocational Behavior, 68*, 474-489.

Quirke, B. (2000). *Making the connections: Using internal communication to turn strategy into action*. Burlington, VT: Gower Publishing Company.

Shannon, J. (2002). *73 Ways to improve your employee communication program*. Glen Rock, NJ: Davis & Company.

Smith, L. (2005). *Effective internal communication*. Sterling, VA: Kogan Page.

Soupata, L. (2005). Engaging employees in company success: The UPS approach to a winning team. *Human Resource Management, 44*, 95-98.

Vandenberg, R. J., Richardson, H., & Eastman, L. (1999). The impact of high involvement organizations: Their antecedents and consequences. *Groups and Organization Management, 24*, 300-339.

CLUSTER M: COLLABORATING ACROSS BOUNDARIES

If we are together nothing is impossible. If we are divided all will fail.
Sir Winston Churchill – British Prime Minister
and winner of the Nobel Prize in Literature

If you can run the company a bit more collaboratively, you get a better result,
because you have more bandwidth and checking and balancing going on.
Larry Page – Co-founder, Google

THE SIGNPOST

Synergy—probably an overused term, but that doesn't minimize its importance. Effective organizations have learned how to leverage cooperation and collaboration. To what extent is the organization given to turfsmanship? Do people protect their sandbox? Are egos swollen and protective of fiefdoms? The extent to which organizations promote collaboration across boundaries can impact the quality of decisions and the speed with which decisions are made. Collaboration can enhance buy-in, give employees a sense of ownership, and facilitate change. The whole is greater than the sum of the parts.

ITEMS

13. Work well in teams when required
33. Support teams where critical and appropriate
53. Use cross-functional/unit work teams and task forces to address problems
73. Seamlessly coordinate work across boundaries (departments, functions, geographies, and business)
87. Move decision-making authority as close to the action as possible
93. Effectively work through internal conflicts with minimum damage

UNSKILLED

- Doesn't clearly define and communicate strategic objectives
- Fails to communicate the value of collaboration
- Only rewards individual contribution
- Staffs teams ineffectively; doesn't ensure adequate skill coverage
- Doesn't build a culture of trust and cooperation
- Fails to provide adequate resources for teams
- Doesn't empower teams to make decisions and take action
- Creates ineffective team metrics
- Fails to hold teams accountable
- Is intolerant of diversity

SKILLED

- Clearly communicates strategic intent and shared goals
- Passionately creates a culture of trust and teamwork
- Excels at talent assessment and team staffing decisions
- Values and promotes diversity of perspectives and backgrounds
- Promotes teamwork through communication and reward systems
- Provides wide availability of team building and conflict-management training
- Allocates resources appropriately to ensure team success
- Embraces ideas from all sources; not wedded to the past
- Creates team processes that address decision making, authority, and metrics
- Sets high standards for team achievement and holds teams accountable

SOME CAUSES

- Pervasive distrust
- Lack of strategic clarity
- Dysfunctional reward system
- Narrow perspective; intolerance
- Inadequately developed team processes
- Conflict not managed
- Impatience with group processes
- Dominant individual personalities and leadership styles

THE TEN LEADERSHIP ARCHITECT® COMPETENCIES MOST ASSOCIATED WITH THIS CLUSTER (in order of connectedness)

33. Listening

18. Delegation

27. Informing

12. Conflict Management

42. Peer Relationships

36. Motivating Others

39. Organizing

41. Patience

60. Building Effective Teams

56. Sizing Up People

THE MAP

Working up and down the organization has always been easier than working across. There are natural barriers that prevent cross-group relationships and communication. Early studies in the social psychology of groups have documented the tendency for groups to be less than cooperative or helpful across teams. There is more competition than cooperation. There is more hoarding than sharing. There is more hiding than showing. But global competition and technology development continue to accelerate. Increasingly complex problems and challenges can best be addressed through collaboration across the hierarchical silos that exist in most organizations. Creative synergies and breakthrough thinking are being driven less by conventional wisdom and best practices and more by real-time, asynchronous, informal communication networks. Seldom do all the answers reside in one vertical unit of the organization. Organizations are becoming webs of free-flowing information and collaboration. New theories, strategies, and technologies have emerged. Blogging, podcasting, virtual networking, open source software, and global communications networks are rewriting the rules of competitive strategy and work process. Egos, turf protection, and control are giving way to electronically-enabled social networks and temporary, multidisciplined, geographically-dispersed talent pools. Money is flowing to the smartest, most creative, and quickest, both inside and outside traditional hierarchical structures. Enterprises that once competed are now leveraging unique capabilities. Collaboration, relationship building, authority sharing, joint ownership, and discipline in team leadership are becoming the new leadership skills. Collaboration is not a fad. Its importance is not going to fade. Collaboration is in!

SOME REMEDIES

1. **Set expectations for collaboration.** The research is in: Groups are smarter than individuals. James Surowiecki, in *The Wisdom of Crowds*, shows that when it comes to decision making, group thinking produces better outcomes than individuals on their own. What you might sacrifice in terms of time you will get back many times over in outcomes. Significant innovations inside organizations are best implemented through cooperation and collaboration. A group that has created the solution together is more likely to band together to implement it successfully. What beliefs does your leadership harbor about heroic individualism or death-by-committee? Both are deadly. Study your own history! Make a list of the breakthrough ideas, new products, services, and processes developed in your organization during the last few years. How many were successfully implemented by an individual, solitary genius? How many were the result of integrating and orchestrating the efforts of individuals and teams across the enterprise? What is the economic value of the goods and services these collaborations have produced? Why would anyone do anything other than collaborate? Have a formal stated viewpoint on collaboration. Make it one of the values of the organization.

2. **Reward collaboration.** Most organizational systems (staffing, performance management, compensation, succession, etc.) are designed to reinforce the efforts and impact of the individual. We have made heroes of the loner, the maverick, the genius, and yet, most enduring legacy rests on the orchestration

of group work, cooperation, and collaboration. Over time, organizations that win are going to have to balance the support, recognition, and rewards for teams and collaboration with the transitional emphasis on the individual. Take, for instance, rewards and recognition. People pay attention to what's measured. Behaviors that are positively recognized and reinforced get repeated. You get what you pay for. The trail of failed or inconsistent collaborative efforts often winds its way through organizations that talk team but reward mostly individual results. Audit your reward system. What percentage of work is being done and results achieved through collaborative efforts? Move an appropriate percentage of spot rewards, merit pay, bonuses, and stock grants away from rewarding individual results to rewards for collaborative behaviors and achievements. Find a balance that rewards stars for their singular impact and teams for their collaborative impact. Stop automatic payouts by level that have no behavioral anchors. Audit your recognition system. Whom do you recognize as heroes and why? Find success stories of collaboration and communicate them consistently. Audit your promotion system. Who gets promoted and why? Competency research provides evidence that promotion is largely based on individual skills (initiative, perseverance, smarts) and not on collaborative skills. Promote people into leadership who demonstrate the willingness and capacity for team building.

3. **Remove barriers.** Not all work is best done by a group, but it is hard to imagine a process that can't be improved through collaboration. Relentlessly identifying barriers, sacred cows, and protected turf is the key. Bring a diverse group of people representing three age generations (Boomer, Gen X, and Gen Y) together to identify the failures, inhibitors, enablers, and benefits of collaboration. What is being protected? Why? By whom? Ask people relatively new to the organization. Create plans to remove barriers and follow through to destroy them.

4. **Use technology to enable networks.** *The World Is Flat* by Thomas Friedman provides one of the best explanations of how fundamental changes in technology have made real-time collaboration on a global scale a reality. No time to read a book? Google "The World Is Flat, Thomas Friedman" and you will get more than three million reviews, articles, summaries, blogs, podcasts, and video interviews to choose from to get up-to-speed. Today the average twelve-year-old is using technology for social networking that the average executive doesn't even know exists. Discover what it means to remove all barriers of time and distance from social networking and collaboration. Start using the technology that enables networking and collaboration in the organization. Get your people connected. Better yet, don't stand in the way. People around the world are dismantling barriers to the free flow of ideas and interactivity. The old ways are being replaced by informal, spontaneous, proactive networks where people inside and outside the organization mingle and collaborate, unrestrained by corporate mandate or control. The secret is to learn to tap this social energy for competitive advantage.

Encourage, support, and invest in instant messaging, podcasting, blogging, social dialogue, and inter-company brainstorming. Create competitions to spur creative application of social networking technology. Sponsor the winners in expanding efforts to include larger portions of the enterprise.

5. **Foster trust across boundaries.** The vast majority of people are trusting and can be trusted. Yet organizations often have pockets of dysfunction where doubting, antagonistic, and uncooperative behavior reigns. Power struggles between organizational disciplines are crippling and costly. Unnecessary competition can and should be replaced by mutual understanding and respect. Face problems head-on. Shine a light on them. Do what it takes to resolve them. If necessary, bring in a specialist in Appreciative Inquiry, Difficult Conversations, or some other procedural model to identify the sources of mistrust and dysfunction. Sponsor small group, cross-functional teams and task forces to work together, separated from the centers of negative influence (often the functional leaders themselves). Recognize and reward those rising stars who foster trust and know how to collaborate. Create a culture that encourages everyone's contribution, cross-pollinates diverse perspectives, and cultivates collective intelligence. Organize for collaboration. Identify the structural barriers to collaboration and redesign them. Think radical redesign. Do you want research, design, purchasing, and manufacturing to work together? Put them together in teams where their ONLY office is a shared conference room with small adjacent phone rooms. Want operations and staff functions to collaborate? Create small, cross-functional groups from the frontline to the executive suite where ALL decisions are based on recommendations made by these groups.

6. **Build conflict-resolution skills.** The dark side of collaboration is the inevitable conflict that arises when goals conflict, egos clash, pressure mounts, patience wears thin, and tempers fly. Up-front statements to emphasize the convergence of interests, equity in values, and appreciation for a diversity of viewpoints can help reduce potential conflict. Recognize the realities of your culture. An impatient, controlling leadership culture will tend to generate more conflict. Once conflict has surfaced, the remedies are clear. Clarify common ground. Encourage dialogue rather than debate. Uncover the underlying "undiscussable" issues. Clearly and specifically articulate the problems. Resolve misunderstandings. Depersonalize the conflict. Don't hold a grudge. Allow people to save face. Encourage small concessions. Synthesize dilemmas. Rather than adopt either/or solutions, look for a third option. Use a mediator if necessary. Work on group conflict-management skills. Create a course. Bring in an expert on conflict resolution to address top management.

7. **Work on organizational patience.** Leaders set the tone. Many are impatient speed demons. Collaboration usually does take more time than going it alone. Sustained winning is the goal, and speed is only part of the game. Quality,

87

innovation, repeat customers, and profitability are other important components of success. A team or task force leader who doesn't have patience for team processes can chill the innovation and quality of collaborative work. Let the team or task force set the bar and establish expectations for the project. Go for the best solution to the problem, not the first. Research says somewhere between the second and third solution is often the best. Go for the most creative idea, not the first. Give collaboration adequate time to work.

8. **Document the economic value of collaboration.** Does collaboration provide any economic value? The way an executive team answers this question may have a lot to do with the level of support provided to teams, task forces, and collaboration. A common complaint is that, "The task force didn't accomplish anything." How do you ensure that the economic value of collaboration is realized? Understand the purpose of any proposed collaborative effort. Set supportive and realistic expectations for collaboration. Have the workgroup set specific goals and objectives for itself. Give teams the resources they need to achieve their goals. Make all collaborative work focused on achievements, on outcomes. If the work product of a collaborative effort is a recommendation, judge the quality of the recommendation. Use team rewards. Promote into leadership positions people who know how to collaborate.

9. **Provide team training.** Dozens of high-performing team models with supporting training programs exist. Pick one. Train managers in collaboration and team processes, group facilitation skills, and developing peer relations. Assess and give feedback on teaming skills. Monitor and measure group effectiveness and impact. Reward teams for group results.

10. **Delegate and relinquish control.** Organizations don't collaborate, people do. Organizations don't resist collaboration, overcontrolling leaders do. Maintaining control is comforting. Letting go is scary. Trusting groups to produce breakthrough ideas or process improvements on their own can be unnerving. Behind every failed attempt to team is a manager who can't let go, is fearful of group failure, is ignorant of team work processes, feels devalued because he doesn't know how to contribute as a team leader, or is certain he has the best ideas and answers. Don't make collaboration optional. All the skills of a great collaborator are learned through collaboration.

11. **Add collaboration competencies to executive and management success profiles.** Add the ten competencies listed above to the assessment and evaluation processes in your organization. Address them in hiring, development, and succession planning. Use them for job assignments and promotions. Give people feedback on them. Have course offerings for each of them. People who possess a critical amount of those ten competencies tend to be better collaborators than those without.

SUGGESTED READINGS

Ashkenas, R., Ulrich, D., Jick, T., & Kerr, S. (1995). *The boundaryless organization: Breaking the chains of organizational structure.* San Francisco, CA: Jossey-Bass.

Bennis, W. G., & Biederman, P. W. (1998). *Organizing genius: The secrets of creative collaboration.* New York, NY: Perseus Books Group.

Beyerlein, M. M., Johnson, D. A., & Beyerlein, S. T. (2004). *Complex collaboration: Building the capabilities for working across boundaries.* Amsterdam, Netherlands: Elsevier.

Druskat, V. U., & Wheeler, J. V. (2003). Managing from the boundary: The effective leadership of self-managing work teams. *Academy of Management Journal, 46*(4), 435-457.

Friedman, T. L. (2006). *The world is flat: A brief history of the twenty-first century.* New York, NY: Farrar, Straus and Giroux.

Gerzon, M., (2006). *Leading through conflict: How successful leaders transform differences into opportunities.* Boston, MA: Harvard Business School Press.

Gooderham, P. N., & Nordhaug, O. (Eds.). (2003). *International management: Cross-boundary challenges.* Malden, MA: Blackwell Publishing Inc.

Hambrick, D. C. (1987). The top management team: Key to strategic success. *California Management Review, 30*(1), 88-100.

Jeannet, J. (2000). *Managing with a global mindset.* Upper Saddle River, NJ: Financial Times/Prentice Hall.

Lawler, E. (2000). *From the ground up: Six principles for building the new logic corporation.* San Francisco, CA: Jossey-Bass.

Lencioni, P. M. (2006). *Silos, politics and turf wars: A leadership fable about destroying the barriers that turn colleagues into competitors.* San Francisco: Jossey-Bass.

Linden, R. M. (2002). *Working across boundaries: Making collaboration work in government and nonprofit organizations.* Hoboken, NJ: John Wiley & Sons, Inc.

Parker, G. M. (2002). *Cross-functional teams: Working with allies, enemies, and other strangers.* Hoboken, NJ: Jossey-Bass.

Surowiecki, J. (2005). *The Wisdom of Crowds.* New York, NY: Anchor Books.

M: COLLABORATION

DIMENSION V: LEVERAGING A PRODUCTIVE CULTURE

CLUSTER N: MANAGING DIVERSITY

He who is different from me does not impoverish me – he enriches me.
Antoine de Saint-Exupéry – French writer and aviator

If man is to survive, he will have learned to take a delight
in the essential differences between men and between cultures.
He will learn that differences in ideas and attitudes are a delight,
part of life's exciting variety, not something to fear.
Gene Roddenberry – Producer and creator of Star Trek

THE SIGNPOST

Ideally, the diversity of an organization mirrors the diversity of its customer population. If you're a global enterprise, your organization should represent global diversity. Diversity leads to new perspectives and new approaches. Homogenous organizations may have less conflict to manage, though this can't be taken for granted, but they lose out from the contribution of a variety of backgrounds, experiences, and approaches to problem solving.

ITEMS

14. Have the diversity in our workforce and among top decision makers that aligns with the labor market and our customers
34. Make effective use of diversity (of thought, opinion, gender, ethnicity, etc.) in our workforce
54. Anticipate and effectively adjust for demographic changes and diversity in our workforce

UNSKILLED

- Avoids diversity issues and opportunities
- Views diversity as a compliance or social requirement
- Provides no or superficial diversity training
- Holds people of diversity to a double standard
- Has only addressed diversity at low position levels; executive ranks are not diverse
- Sees diversity as a cause of problems, not as part of the solution
- Fails to address diversity-related conflicts
- Does not promote an inclusionary culture that is attractive to people of diversity

- Holds narrow views as to what constitutes diversity; doesn't recognize customer diversity
- Has not deployed diversity to address significant business issues

SKILLED

- Fosters an inclusionary, tolerant, respectful culture that celebrates diversity
- Establishes policies and programs to reflect a rich diversity viewpoint
- Actively recruits and promotes to achieve diversity at all levels in the organization
- Faces diversity-related conflicts head-on and uses them as opportunities for learning
- Takes a broad, inclusive view; values, respects, and appreciates diversity of all kinds
- Has the same high expectations for people of diversity as for others
- Effectively deploys diversity to solve meaningful business problems
- Actively seeks a workforce composition that mirrors marketplace diversity
- Implements rigorous diversity training; promotes learning transfer to the work environment
- Consistently reinforces diversity values through communication and actions

SOME CAUSES

- Narrow perspective
- Cultural ignorance
- Entrenched prejudices and stereotypes
- Conflict avoidance
- Fear of change, the different, the unknown
- Organizational arrogance
- Organizational defensiveness
- Mired in traditions or the past

THE TEN LEADERSHIP ARCHITECT® COMPETENCIES MOST ASSOCIATED WITH THIS CLUSTER (in order of connectedness)

21. Managing Diversity
25. Hiring and Staffing
46. Perspective
56. Sizing Up People
58. Strategic Agility
2. Dealing with Ambiguity
64. Understanding Others
19. Developing Direct Reports and Others
33. Listening
36. Motivating Others

THE MAP

There can be joy in differences. Differences can enhance. Differences can energize. Differences can add value. On the other hand, for some, differences can complicate. They might be scary. They might slow things down. They might lead to conflict. So, some people seek out and welcome differences while others avoid and shy away from diversity. Organizations, too, differ in their willingness and ability to comprehend, appreciate, and use diversity. They differ in how they value diversity. It does everyone in the organization a disservice to strive for diversity simply out of a sense of social obligation or an effort to comply with an externally imposed or self-imposed quota. Embrace diversity not only because it's the right thing to do. Embrace diversity because it provides a competitive advantage. When diversity is leveraged to solve real problems, the benefits are enormous. And tapping into the benefits of diversity is getting easier every day. Immigration, changing world demographics, the globalization of markets and businesses, and technological innovations all have contributed to an increasingly diverse workforce and customer base. The world is changing and getting more diverse, and successful organizations mirror this change. Their policies are inclusive of differences and consider global diversity. Their business strategy is aligned with diversity strategy and capitalizes on differing perspectives to innovate, improve products and services, and reach new markets. They have an increased awareness of personal and organizational values and an acknowledgement of differences in perspective. They don't fear differences—they view differences as an asset that leads to innovation, novel problem solving, and opportunities to expand their market. A diverse customer base is best addressed by a diverse workforce led by a diverse management team that genuinely values diversity.

SOME REMEDIES

1. **Conduct a four-way diversity audit.** Find out where you stand. First, take a look at the diversity of your market and customer base. Quantify it. Look to the census information. Look to your customer relationship management (CRM) system if you're using one. Get outside help from a demographer and a market research firm. Second, do the same audit of the labor market for the kinds and types of people you need for your workforce. Work to fill open jobs. Check your applicant flow. Next, do an audit of the communities where you have major facilitates and operations. Lastly, do the same audit of your workforce. Review the findings with top management. Look to the gaps. Set goals and create a plan to get there.

2. **Elevate the importance of diversity.** Create a common mind-set around diversity. Use the broadest view of diversity as you can. Create and communicate the organization's commitment to diversity by crafting a diversity statement. Put diversity content into the mission statement and into the values of the

93

organization. Work diversity into all senior management speeches. Insert it into the branding collateral. Create recruiting brochures around diversity. Put it in the annual report. Have the marketing and PR functions create an ad campaign around it. Put it into evaluation and assessment processes. Reward people and units for accomplishments around diversity goals. Celebrate diversity.

3. **Shape a diversity friendly culture.** Work on the various aspects of a diversity friendly culture:

- **Increase awareness.** Organizations (and the individuals within them) should be aware of closely held beliefs and values. Watch for stereotypes, prejudices, and biases that chill the intelligent use of diversity. This requires examining what is valued and why. Becoming self-aware is necessary to recognize, then to effectively manage and utilize differing perspectives.

- **Adopt flexible thinking and problem solving.** Consider different answers, reasons, or approaches to problems—think differently. Challenge traditional views and thinking—don't suppress unconventional thinking. Do things differently. Open vistas. Take a new look at vexing problems from a diversity of viewpoints.

- **Manage conflict.** Deploying diversity will likely involve conflict management. Diversity inherently presents the potential for conflict— the immediate reaction to different viewpoints and backgrounds is to withdraw or to become defensive. Do not avoid conflict. Encourage individuals to think in shades of gray rather than black-and-white terms. Reflect on the perspectives and values that are at the root of conflict. Acknowledge viewpoints. Deal with emotions. Teach conflict resolution in training courses.

- **Stress substance over style.** The focus of work needs to be accomplishments, rather than style. Different approaches might be used by people with different backgrounds, but different approaches can result in similar (or improved) achievements. Outcomes rule.

- **Challenge stereotypes.** Failing to challenge individuals who use stereotypes, prejudices, and biases is a form of reinforcement and signals acceptance. Challenge stereotypes. Act in ways that break commonly held stereotypes.

- **Encourage open dialogue.** Promoting communication without boundaries, interruption, or fear of ridicule can be a powerful diversity deployment tool and result in greater understanding and connection. It is important that everyone has equal opportunity to engage in open dialogue and no one hogs the stage.

- **Watch double standards.** People need to be judged equitably and similarly. Many times people of diversity need to perform better to be seen as the same. Adjust for differences.

- **Recognize challenges.** Recognize the adversity and challenges that can accompany diversity and deal with them. When the daily language is a second language, for example, some might be hard to understand. It takes effort and patience. Make allowances for differences that are not directly related to job performance. Waiting a few extra minutes for a value-adding suggestion is worth the time.

4. **Make the business case for diversity.** Nothing much will happen until you have the business case in mind for increased diversity in the organization. Are your markets and customers more diverse than your employees? Where are your major new opportunities for volume and share? Are they in your home market? People just like you? Most likely not. Do you know a lot about the people and cultures inside and outside your home country who are going to buy your products and make you successful? As the population becomes more diverse, consider that same-culture sales and marketing people have had more success selling (Hispanics to Hispanics, for example). Innovation is enhanced by diversity. Studies show that heterogeneous or diverse groups are more innovative than homogeneous groups. They view opportunities from different perspectives. The majority of the U.S. labor market will shortly be former minorities. Females and minorities collectively will be in the majority. Companies known in the marketplace for managing diversity well will get their pick of the best and brightest. A broader talent pool means more choices. The most effective managers tend to have a more diverse array of people around them. The rest will get the leftovers. Are you known for managing diversity well? Want increased motivation and productivity? There is a positive relationship between perceived equity/feeling valued and the performance of organizations. The business case boils down to more perspectives, more chances to learn, more ways to appeal to different market segments, and a more productive workforce where all employees think merit is what counts in an organization.

5. **Establish diversity metrics.** Measure progress toward diversity goals. Measure diversity in the broadest possible sense. Design a comprehensive set of measurements that tracks hiring (applications and placement), promotions, high potentials, development plans and achievement, engagement, retention, and deployment. Put the measurements into goals and objectives for HR and for line management. Publish progress against the goals.

6. **Address diversity in on-boarding.** People who are significantly different in any observable way will typically find it difficult to fit into a group of people who don't share that difference. Create a program that aids people of diversity to more easily and comfortably integrate into the organization. Assimilation of diversity

into most organizations presents unique problems. Create an on-boarding process with special attention to the unique challenges faced by people of diversity. With smoother assimilation and integration come increased productivity and an increased chance of retention.

7. **Work on the diversity experience.** Provide top management with plenty of opportunities to experience and learn about diversity. Bring in speakers of diversity. Have meetings in diverse settings and locations. Sponsor diversity events. Fund the diversity efforts of nonprofits. Encourage executives to volunteer time and expertise to diversity-related programs. Have executives attend festivals to observe and report back on the context for diversity.

8. **Deploy diversity effectively.** Deploy people of diversity in a variety of roles, levels, and functions. Make sure that task forces, project teams, and study groups are diverse. Make sure that training classes and off-site workshops are diverse. Use special assignments to get a diversity of viewpoints working on vexing problems.

9. **Communicate and celebrate diversity successes.** Look for and document how the diversity of project teams enhanced outcomes. Collect and communicate stories and anecdotes about where and how diversity of any kind added value to performance and results.

10. **Recruit for diversity.** Organizations that are diverse find it easiest to attract people of diversity. The converse is true for organizations that lack diversity, and they must place special effort to establish a diversity presence. Fortunately, there are well-documented best practices for successful diversity recruiting. If you're far from where you should be, if you're behind your competition, you need to place extra emphasis on implementing a best practices recruiting process.

SUGGESTED READINGS

Bassett-Jones, N. (2005). The paradox of diversity management, creativity and innovation. *Creativity and Innovation Management, 14*, 169-175.

Bucher, R. A., & Bucher, P. L. (2003). *Diversity consciousness: Opening our minds to people, cultures, and opportunities* (2nd ed.). Upper Saddle River, NJ: Prentice Hall.

Carr-Ruffino, N. (2005). *Managing diversity: People skills for a multicultural workplace* (7th ed.). Boston, MA: Pearson Custom Publishing.

Cox, T., Jr. (2001). *Creating the multicultural organization: A strategy for capturing the power of diversity.* San Francisco: Jossey-Bass.

Earley, P. C., & Ang, S. (2003). *Cultural intelligence: Individual interactions across cultures. Stanford,* CA: Stanford University Press.

Fowler, S. M. (2006). Training across cultures: What intercultural trainers bring to diversity training. *International Journal of Intercultural Relations, 30*, 401-411.

Gardenswatz, L., & Rowe, A. (1992). *Managing diversity: A complete desk reference and planning guide.* New York, NY: McGraw-Hill.

Harvey, C., & Allard, M. J. (2004). *Understanding and managing diversity* (3rd ed.). Upper Saddle River, NJ: Prentice Hall.

Hubbard, E. E. (2003). *The diversity scorecard: Evaluating the impact of diversity on organizational performance (Improving human performance).* Burlington, MA: Elsevier Butterworth-Heinemann.

Kilian, C. M., Hukai, D., & McCarty, C. E. (2005). Building diversity in the pipeline to corporate leadership. *Journal of Management Development, 24*, 155-168.

Marx, E. (1999). *Breaking through culture shock: What you need to succeed in international business.* London, UK: Nicholas Brealey Publishing.

Mor Barak, M. (2005). *Managing diversity: Toward a globally inclusive workplace.* Thousand Oaks, CA: Sage Publications, Inc.

Peterson, B. (2004). *Cultural intelligence: A guide to working with people from other cultures.* Yarmouth, ME: Intercultural Press, Inc.

Thomas, D. C., & Inkson, K. (2004). *Cultural intelligence: People skills for global business.* San Francisco, CA: Berrett-Koehler Publishers, Inc.

Thomas, K. M. (2005). *Diversity dynamics in the workplace.* Belmont, CA: Wadsworth.

Thomas, R. R., Thomas, D. A., Ely, R. J., & Meyerson, D. (2002). *Harvard business review on managing diversity.* Boston, MA: Harvard Business School Press.

CLUSTER O: BASIS FOR COMPETITIVE ADVANTAGE

Drive thy business, let not that drive thee.
Benjamin Franklin – Author, inventor, philosopher, and diplomat

Nothing focuses the mind better than the constant sight of a competitor who wants to wipe you off the map.
Wayne Calloway – Former Chairman and CEO, PepsiCo

THE SIGNPOST
What is the basis for competitive advantage in your organization? Is your focus on quality, customer service, being the low-cost provider? The most effective organizations know they can't be all things to all customers. They are very clear about how they gain competitive advantage.

ITEMS
15. Be the price/value leader in our marketplace
35. Be the low-cost producer or provider in our marketplace
55. Be the premium/quality niche provider
74. Be the customer-service leader in our marketplace
88. Continuously enter, create, and grow new markets

UNSKILLED
- Lacks strategic focus; tries to do too much
- Doesn't closely monitor competitors
- Fails to listen to or survey customers
- Falsely believes an advantage exists when in fact it does not
- Has an advantage, but does not know what it is
- Doesn't communicate competitive advantage to customers
- Sticks with a strategy, even when the evidence says it isn't working
- Fails to adopt a strategy aligned with organizational capabilities
- Executes the selected strategy poorly
- Is slow to recognize disruptions in the market

SKILLED
- Creates a focused strategy aligned with customers and organizational capabilities
- Maintains an intimate connection with customers and acts on feedback
- Closely monitors competitors and knows their strategies

99

- Communicates competitive advantage clearly to customers
- Executes flawlessly with attention to detail and follow-through
- Responds quickly and with great agility to adjust to changes in the business landscape
- Engages employees to target their energies in building competitive advantage
- Possesses clarity of purpose and focuses resources and energy appropriately
- Establishes metrics and reward systems that measure and reinforce the strategic intent

SOME CAUSES

- Narrow perspective; inwardly focused
- Lack of strategic focus
- Organizational arrogance
- Rigid; slow to adapt
- Poor listening
- No continuity; churn at the top of the organization
- Mixed messages
- Dysfunctional culture
- Doesn't use customer or competitor data well
- Short-term view

THE TEN LEADERSHIP ARCHITECT® COMPETENCIES MOST ASSOCIATED WITH THIS CLUSTER (in order of connectedness)

15. Customer Focus
53. Drive for Results
63. Total Work Systems (e.g., TQM/ISO/Six Sigma)
 5. Business Acumen
50. Priority Setting
24. Functional/Technical Skills
28. Innovation Management
51. Problem Solving
16. Timely Decision Making
52. Process Management

THE MAP

Successful organizations are clear about who they are. No identity crisis. They know who their customers are. They're clear about differences—differences in their products, services, organizational capabilities, values, and execution. Though they maintain openness to ideas from any source, they're not copycats. They adopt ideas and best practices from others not out of conformism but out of a desire to be even more differentiated. They know that competitive advantage comes through distinction.

100

Distinction, differentiation can take many forms: in product—features, design aesthetics, usability, simplicity, serviceability, durability, etc.; in distribution—retail outlets, wholesale outlets, franchises, online, etc.; in marketing channels—direct mail, telemarketing, cybermarketing, radio, TV, cable, billboards, etc. The possibilities for differentiation are almost endless when you consider the permutations offered through branding, pricing, sales, engineering, distribution, service, packaging, advertising, promotion, customization, and so forth. So how do you decide? Listen to your customers, carefully analyze the complex and comprehensive business landscape, and play to your strengths. Align your competitive strategy with those things and in a way that sets you apart from the competition. Read Porter's strategy books and those by Treacy and Wiersema. Contrast their ideas with those of Hamel and Prahalad and of Kim and Mauborgne. Adopt a competitive strategy. Get clear about it. Communicate it. Execute it.

SOME REMEDIES

1. **Choose the right strategy.** Do one thing better than anyone else, rather than trying to do everything as well as everyone else. Consumers need to have an obvious reason to choose your organization's products and services. You need to look at three things. First, what does your organization do especially well? If your organization doesn't think about the organization in terms of its core capabilities, get started. Start by having everyone in top management read three books and articles on the subject. Have each member of management report on what they have read. Collect the lessons and produce a report on how all of this applies to your organization. Bring in a top core competency consultant to help get top management educated. Audit your capabilities. Do a core capability survey. Which strategy best fits your organization? There are a number of commercially available surveys you can use. Have top management and one level below them complete the survey. Produce a report and have a core capability off-site to discuss the results. Be careful about developing arrogance around what you're best at. Second, what does the customer want? You can differentiate your customers just like you can differentiate products and services. There are cheap customers, luxury customers, and customers who want everything fast. What portion of the market do you want? Are there enough buyers in your category to go around? Third, what are your competitors doing? Some are probably well defined and doing it well while others are struggling to find their way. What part of the market are your competitors after? Once you select a strategy, embed it into the culture— low-cost provider employees share office supplies and suggest cost-saving strategies; quality-first employees dress to impress; the customer-service leader CEO is gregarious and visible—he/she treats everyone as special. An organization cannot typically be the low-cost provider as well as the customer-service leader

and industry innovator. The focus of the organization has to be understood and communicated to all stakeholders, internal and external. Embrace the source of advantage—it is what makes you unique. The business literature is filled with "how to" information about how to operate across the different strategies.

2. **Constantly scan the business landscape.** Know what's going on in your industry and market. Every competitor should be charted as primarily striving for low cost, quality, innovation, or customer service. If you have a difficult time charting the competition's strategy, so do consumers. Have sensors/feelers that can communicate quickly with key decision makers. Know how the market is behaving and why. Solicit feedback from consumers—use anonymous surveys. Ask for information. Have regular meetings with front-line employees—know what's going on at the customer touch points. Pay attention to investor behavior and the local, regional, and larger economy. There is no such thing as too much information. Adapt and change quickly as the business landscape changes. Strategies are not forever.

3. **Anticipate what's next.** Predict change. Plan for it. Will your source of competitive advantage be effective in emerging international markets? With younger customers? Older consumers? With multicultural and multilingual consumers? Build contingency plans to meet changing markets and environmental conditions. If the economy takes a dip, will the innovative strategy be as effective? If changes are anticipated, it is easier to be flexible and adaptive.

4. **Size up the competition.** Know who the competition is and what strategies they employ. Monitor the environment for fringe-players—organizations that might creep into your market. Understand potential foreign competition. Potential competition is tougher to monitor than existing competition, but just as important. Know the fringe-industries. Know what the competition is doing and why. Who are their key customers and how do they differ from yours? How successful are they? How are their profits charting? What's their market share? Projected market share? How successful is their strategy? Once again, there is no such thing as too much information. Run scenarios that consider new competitive entrants into your space. What will you do if they shift into your niche? How will you respond to an invasion into your customer base? What can you do to erect barriers to entry or confound new entrants? What can you do to distract them from a competing strategy? Can you take them on in their own game? Create a diverse team to plan scenarios against each of your major competitors. The team should be responsible for learning everything they can about that organization. They should periodically report back to top management on what the competitor is doing now and what they are most likely to do in the future. When you are contemplating a shift in your strategy, they will study the expected changes and try to predict competitor moves. Gaining competitive advantage is a contact sport—as much football as it

is chess. The pursuit of market share leads to a dog-eat-dog mentality. It is not necessary to view the situation as ruthless, but no one should expect gains to be made without challenge. Assume competitors know as much as you know—the difference is in the execution. Your goal is to take the same information and execute better than others do.

5. **Keep in touch with stakeholders.** Know what customers expect from your organization and your industry. Know how your employees view and buy into your strategy. Anonymous employee and customer surveys can be fairly easy to administer. Know who your key customers are and act on their needs. Are the return customers aware of your strategy or simply making choices based on convenience (i.e., location)? Track your effectiveness in gaining competitive advantage—what's the market share trend? If you don't have one, consider a CRM (customer relationship management) system to help you make better decisions about serving customers.

6. **Remove obstacles to strategy.** If your source of competitive advantage is innovation, encourage open dialogue and tolerate failures. If the source is low-cost advantage, remove as much overhead as possible. If the source is customer focus, ensure that the voice of the customer does not get blocked through chains of escalation. Once a strategic direction is chosen, do an internal audit on potential roadblocks. Make sure employees are aware of the strategic focus. A lack of awareness is a large potential obstacle to any strategic plan. The organization culture and operating systems need to match the strategy.

7. **Maintain the balance between established and new relationships.** Always consider new markets but never to the neglect of existing markets. Firmly establish your value proposition in the market. Not every customer will be able to articulate why they choose one provider over another. Spell it out for them. If they know, they can recruit other like-minded customers. When you solicit feedback from customers, make sure you follow up to express appreciation and let them know what's being done with the information. Consider preferred-consumer programs—anything to build a relationship between existing consumers and your organization. On the other hand, look to open new markets and get more customers. Make sure you do not muddy your strategy in the hunt for new customers. Companies have suffered in the past by confusing their current customers while trying to get new ones. Offering a cheaper alternative to a previous quality product may actually cost you high-end customers. If you are going to try a two-tiered offering, carefully consider how it can be positioned in the market without causing confusion. Will the customers who pay more be irritated when the cheaper, faster version comes on the market in another channel?

8. **Align your culture.** What do you care about? What do you believe about the business? About your customers? About employees? What do you want to achieve? What behaviors do you want to promote your competitive advantage? The culture that promotes those behaviors is an aligned and effective culture. It will shape how all stakeholders—customers, employees, investors—and the rest of the world perceive the organization. If your competitive strategy is speed, consider how your culture promotes that characteristic. How do you talk about speed? How do you reward it? How do you celebrate it? How are decisions made? How do policies and procedures impact speed of decision making? What about the organization structure? Anything and everything that impacts behaviors related to speed should be considered and addressed. You can put reminders in the environment—slogans and banners—but it's the behaviors of your top leaders that really send the message. Reinforce your competitive strategy constantly and consistently in communication.

9. **Practice constructive discontent.** You can always improve. It's great to celebrate accomplishments. It's dangerous to rest on your laurels. Complacency spells doom. If the current market is saturated and stagnating, find emerging markets. If emerging markets are not found, you are not looking hard enough (or in the right place). Project how well your strategy will play out in five years, ten years. The war is never won. You can only win battles. Never stop battling. Never think you've won the war. Things change. Consumer preferences shift over time. Technology changes. Business models change. You'll be hit with change. Stay agile and innovative to ensure you're there for battles far into the future.

10. **Map people to the strategy.** Just as your organization is a better fit for some customers than others, it's also a better fit for some employees than others. Some people work better in low-cost operations. They are naturally cost-sensitive and prone to measure and trim expenses. They like things lean. People in enhanced customer-service environments spend money to manage and keep customers. They spend as much time as required to satisfy the customer. They make exceptions to policies to get things done. They are naturally inclined to listen. A high-quality orientation takes a somewhat different skill set. A focus on production another. Speed another. So the people requirements of each strategy are a bit different. Be clear on your strategic intent. Match the people to the strategy.

SUGGESTED READINGS

Christensen, C. M., Roth, E. A., & Anthony, S. D. (2004). *Seeing what's next: Using theories of innovation to predict industry change*. Boston, MA: Harvard Business School Press.

Gottfredson, M., & Aspinall, K. (2005, November). Innovation vs. complexity. *Harvard Business Review, 83*(11), 62-71.

Hamel, G., & Prahalad, C. K. (1996). *Competing for the future*. Boston, MA: Harvard Business School Press.

Kim, W. C., & Mauborgne, R. (2005). *Blue ocean strategy: How to create uncontested market space and make competition irrelevant*. Boston, MA: Harvard Business School Press.

Moore, G. A. (2005, December). Strategy and your stronger hand. *Harvard Business Review, 83*(12), 62-72.

Porter, M. E. (1998a). *Competitive advantage: Creating and sustaining superior performance*. New York, NY: Free Press.

Porter, M. E. (1998b). *Competitive strategy: Techniques for analyzing industries and competitors*. New York: Free Press.

Smith, J. L., & Flanagan, W. G. (2006). *Creating competitive advantage: Give customers a reason to choose you over your competitors*. New York: Currency.

Treacy, M., & Wiersema, F. (1997). *The discipline of market leaders: Choose your customers, narrow your focus, dominate your market*. New York, NY: Perseus Books Group.

Trout, J., & Rivkin, S. (2000). *Differentiate or die: Survival in our era of killer competition*. New York, NY: John Wiley & Sons, Inc.

Ulwick, A. (2005). *What customers want: Using outcome-driven innovation to create breakthrough products and services*. New York, NY: McGraw-Hill.

Whiteley, R., & Hessan, D. (1996). *Customer-centered growth: Five proven strategies for building competitive advantage*. New York, NY: The Forum Corporation.

CLUSTER P: SUPPLY CHAIN MANAGEMENT (FROM RAW MATERIAL TO CUSTOMER)

An army marches on its stomach.
Napoleon Bonaparte – French general and emperor

We're all working together; that's the secret.
Sam Walton – Founder, Wal-Mart

THE SIGNPOST

The supply chain is the network of all the suppliers and distributors that work with the business to supply raw materials, deliver final goods and services to the customer, and provide post-sales service and warranty. The importance of supply chain management has become prominent over the past 20 years as some of the world's most successful organizations have made it the centerpiece of their business model and turned their industries upside down through innovative and aggressive approaches to managing the supply chain.

ITEMS

16. Use our edge in supply chain management to compete
36. Have a set of metrics to monitor our supply chain efficiently and effectively
56. Have more effective supplier and vendor relationships than our competitors
75. Seek out and make joint ventures and strategic partnerships work

UNSKILLED

- Fails to recognize strategic importance of the supply chain
- Lacks acumen to effectively forecast, manage inventory, schedule, etc.
- Takes a short-range view in supply chain decisions; doesn't see downstream impact
- Does not build win-win alliances with suppliers
- Selects technology solutions poorly and has clumsy execution
- Does not implement appropriate metrics to monitor supply chain effectiveness
- Fails to recognize market shifts, technology innovations, and new business models
- Doesn't understand the nature of costs in the supply chain; fails to manage costs
- Employs inadequate information systems; doesn't wring value from information
- Selects inappropriate models; doesn't design the supply chain to match the business model

P: SUPPLY CHAIN

DIMENSION VI: MANAGING PROFITABILITY AND DELIVERING VALUE

SKILLED

- Creates an effective supply chain strategy that provides a compelling competitive advantage
- Optimizes inventory to minimize capital employed and to ensure availability for the customer
- Locates facilities to add value to supply chain efficiency
- Employs optimum transportation means to assure timely delivery while minimizing costs
- Forges win-win alliances with suppliers and distributors
- Continuously improves processes; removes friction that slows processes and drives up costs
- Mines data sources to analyze information and spot opportunities for improving supply chain
- Effectively applies technology; is not afflicted by lust for or fear of technology
- Quickly adapts to changes in the business landscape that impact supply chain management
- Integrates marketing and customer service into supply chain management
- Measures everything that matters and makes the measurements transparent to all concerned

SOME CAUSES

- Lack of process discipline
- Insufficient SCM technical knowledge
- Lacks required business acumen for SCM
- Lags in understanding and application of technology
- Lack of trust in supplier relationships
- Poor negotiator and relationship builder
- Doesn't think systematically
- Doesn't understand or anticipate supply chain partner needs

THE TEN LEADERSHIP ARCHITECT® COMPETENCIES MOST ASSOCIATED WITH THIS CLUSTER (in order of connectedness)

39. Organizing
52. Process Management
 5. Business Acumen
37. Negotiating
47. Planning
51. Problem Solving
15. Customer Focus
29. Integrity and Trust

42. Peer Relationships

59. Managing Through Systems

THE MAP

A business is a closed-loop system. It receives inputs, performs processes to add value to the inputs, and provides outputs to customers in the form of goods and services. Customers close the loop by providing feedback and input in the form of cash. Viewed simply, there are three primary inputs to any business: financial capital (investment), human capital (employees), and raw materials (the supplies and information the business transforms into something tangible, something for which a customer is willing to pay). The supply chain network is extensive and includes all the suppliers and distributors that supply inputs to the business and deliver outputs to the customer. Supply chain management (SCM), then, is the planning, organizing, directing, and controlling of this comprehensive network of resources and processes. In addition to the functions traditionally attributed to logistics—procurement, inventory management, and distribution—SCM includes production and includes (or significantly integrates) marketing, product development, and customer service. The importance of SCM has become more prominent over the past 20 years as some of the world's most successful organizations have made it the centerpiece of their business model. Wal-Mart, Dell Computers, and Amazon.com are examples of companies that have radically shaken up their industries primarily through their innovative and aggressive approaches to total SCM. These companies and others have shown that best practices in SCM lead to decreased costs in inventory, facilities, and employed capital; improved customer satisfaction through better availability and selection; improved efficiencies by employing lean processes and cutting-edge technology to remove friction at the transaction points in the supply chain; higher quality from focusing on handoffs and touch points in the supply chain network so risk of mistakes are reduced. Even if it's not the centerpiece of your business model, your organization cannot afford to overlook the critical importance of your supply chain.

SOME REMEDIES

1. **Map supply chain processes.** The first step to improving any process is to understand it. Process mapping is the method to create a detailed graphic of your supply chain that identifies roles, processes, handoffs, and deliverables. This is the big picture of your current state and provides a way to communicate, manage, and improve your supply chain. For each subprocess, ask key questions: Who is the next customer? What does the process deliver to the customer? Who are the suppliers and what do they supply? What are the requirements of inputs and outputs? What, exactly, occurs in the process? When? How do you know it's performed acceptably? Use what you learn to apply business process engineering techniques to simplify processes by reducing whatever makes sense—steps in

P: SUPPLY CHAIN

DIMENSION VI: MANAGING PROFITABILITY AND DELIVERING VALUE

procedures, distances, handoffs, personnel, equipment, and space. Add to the process only to improve quality, productivity, timeliness, or cost. This becomes a continuous improvement activity that is an embedded and ongoing part of the management of your supply chain.

2. **Design supply chain structures and relationships.** Step back from your mapped SCM processes to consider how your organization is structured—reporting relationships, staffing levels, infrastructure, facilities (capacity and location, capital equipment), and everything else that impacts the performance of the process. Design your organization and infrastructures to support your processes.

3. **Build supply chain technical expertise.** Staffing and development are key to SCM. You need to have (or have access to) people who have the technical skills that are needed by all the functions of SCM—procurement, facilities management, inventory management, forecasting, production, information technology, distribution, material handling, transportation, etc. SCM is a complex process and takes time to learn. To develop staff, check out the opportunities provided by professional organizations such as the Association for Operations Management (still referred to as APICS after its former name, the American Production and Inventory Control Society), Council for Supply Chain Management Professionals, National Association of Purchasing Management, Council of Logistics Management, International Warehouse Logistics Association, Logistics Execution Systems Association, Supply-Chain Council, Warehousing Education and Research Council, Institute of Industrial Engineers, Material Handling Industry of America, Society of Manufacturing Engineers, National Association of Manufacturers, etc. Create an SCM organization and staff it with a mixture of external and internal experts and high-potential, learning-agile employees. Have it report sufficiently high in the organization so it can be a member of the strategic team. If done well, this is a staff department that will pay for itself over and over again.

4. **Understand business drivers.** Thoroughly understand all the costs related to the pieces and parts of your supply chain. Consider the amount of capital you have tied up in facilities, inventory, work-in-progress, and equipment. Calculate your capital costs and use the information to make decisions about capital budgeting, outsourcing, and setting goals for SCM. Consider how alternate SCM decisions impact your fixed and variable costs. The analysis required for SCM is extensive: order entry costs; staffing and costs for inspection; parts obsolescence; insurance and taxes; make versus buy decisions; requirements for information technology, etc., etc. Organizations that fail to understand all the business drivers will make suboptimal decisions and lose out to business with more rigorous SCM methods.

5. **Integrate SCM with other business functions.** The organizations that are most effective at SCM take a comprehensive view and include marketing, product development, and customer service. Marketing is the eyes and ears of the business.

Marketing should provide business intelligence that reveals what customers value. How should products and services be delivered? Through what channels? In what format? What level of customer service do they require? What warranty policies will be most effective? How does branding impact the partnerships with suppliers and distributors? Product development is also important. Designers in many industries are accustomed to designing for manufacturability. What about design for deliverability? For serviceability? The form factor employed for a product or service, including the packaging, can have an impact on the cost and efficiency of delivery. Customer service should definitely be part of the SCM equation and is inextricably linked to marketing and product development, as well. Who services the product? How quickly? Where? How are returns handled? These and many related questions impact the design and management of the supply chain.

6. **Get a grasp on technology.** You can't effectively manage your supply chain without technology. Software products abound with applications that range from splintered specialty tools to comprehensive, integrated, enterprise-level product suites. The field is awash in acronyms—ERP, CRM, RFID, SCEM, JIT, EDI are some of the more common. Specialized expertise is required to implement most SCM technology, but business needs and good management practices should guide all technology decisions. The main drivers will be identified as you're designing and improving processes. At each critical point (typically where there is a transaction of some kind) in your supply chain, ask some key questions. What data is required? By whom? How should it be analyzed for decision making? How should it be reported? Can this transaction or process step be automated? When selecting technology, there is another set of questions to ask that are far too numerous to list here. In addition to basic functionality, selection criteria generally deal with user requirements and usability, hardware requirements, compatibility issues, total cost of ownership, vendor reliability and stability, security and privacy, availability and levels of support, delivery model, and documentation.

7. **Build alliances.** You don't have a complete supply chain without partnerships, without collaboration. The most effective supply chains are truly alliances between parties that provide mutual benefits. Win-win relationships. You are likely to have long-term problems if price is your overriding selection criterion for suppliers and distributors. Of course, price is important. But it's also important to select partners that have adequate quality systems, capacity to meet your current and anticipated needs, and core capabilities that serve your strategic objectives. Too often supply chain relationships are lopsided—suppliers that are brutalized by their customer (e.g., continually hammered over price) or organizations that are held hostage by a supplier that possesses an all-too-powerful bargaining chip (e.g., unrealistic contract terms). Such arrangements aren't real partnerships. Your view should be that you're in a long-term business partnership, that you both need to be successful, that you can learn from each other and should. Collaborate. Build

P: SUPPLY CHAIN

DIMENSION VI: MANAGING PROFITABILITY AND DELIVERING VALUE

111

relationships. Demonstrate integrity and trust. Teach each other. Share best practices. Share successes as well as losses. Be responsive and follow through on commitments. Use top-notch people to manage relationships. The major reason alliances fail is poor relationship management at the top. Do these things to build a resilient supply chain that provides enduring competitive advantage.

8. **Benchmark.** It's not enough to look outside your organization. You need to look outside your industry to study and benchmark a variety of SCM practices and models. For instance, if you're in a health care business, you might study the methods of McDonald's, Southwest Airlines, and Honda. Don't stop there. Practice force-fit thinking to see if you can apply SCM practices from those organizations to your business. If you don't, a competitor will; that can lead to an ugly surprise and result in your scrambling to catch up to a new model. Read voraciously. In addition to the suggested readings below, study a variety of business publications with an eye to spot emerging business models and technologies that will impact your business.

9. **Outsource.** SCM implies a certain amount of outsourcing, but what we're referring to here is the outsourcing of the management of your supply chain. A new breed of organizations, third-party logistics providers (or 3PLs, for short), have recently emerged. These companies have specialized SCM expertise. There is almost nothing in your supply chain that you can't outsource. Whether or not this is a good business decision depends on the same analysis you'd perform to determine any other make/buy decision. Just a few of the questions you'll need to answer include: Is this your core capability? If not, should it be? What is the cost/benefit of outsourcing? What are the implications for brand management? For customer service? How does the decision align with long-term strategic objectives of the organization? Early reports say some if not half of outsourcing fails to deliver the planned savings. Again, it depends upon the management of the outsourcing.

10. **Measure.** Measurement makes effective management possible. It provides focus, helps you diagnose problems and identify opportunities, and tells you if changes you make result in the intended improvement. The best metrics are comprehensive (include assessments of quality, productivity, timeliness, and cost) and balanced across the supply chain (overall system, organization, function, and team). You need to measure outputs as well as processes. Measures should be transparent and communicated to all stakeholders. SCM goals should be specific, measurable, achievable (but aggressive), results-focused, and time-bound. Technology is an important enabler of measurement. Business analytic software can be employed to capture data, analyze information, and display reports in easily read, real-time dashboards that monitor system performance.

SUGGESTED READINGS

Baldwin, C., Clark, K. B., Magretta, J., Dyer, J. H., Fisher, M., & Fites, D. V. (Eds.). (2000). *Harvard business review on managing the value chain*. Boston, MA: Harvard Business School Press.

Bolstorff, P., & Rosenbaum, R. (2003). *Supply chain excellence: A handbook for dramatic improvement using the SCOR model*. New York, NY: AMACOM.

Chopra, S., & Meindl, P. (2003). *Supply chain management: Strategy, planning, and operations* (2nd ed.). Upper Saddle River, NJ: Prentice Hall.

Cohen, S., & Roussel, J. (2005). *Strategic supply chain management: The five disciplines for top performance*. New York, NY: McGraw-Hill.

Goldratt, E. (1997). *Critical chain*. Great Barrington, MA: North River Press.

Goldratt, E., & Cox, J. (2004). *The goal: A process of ongoing improvement* (3rd ed.). Great Barrington, MA: North River Press.

Gottfredson, M., Puryear, R., & Phillips, S. (2005, February). Strategic sourcing from periphery to the core. *Harvard Business Review, 83*(2), 132-139.

Gulati, R. (1998). Alliances and networks. *Strategic Management Journal, 19*(4). 293-327.

Handfield, R., & Nichols, E., Jr. (2002). *Supply chain redesign: Transforming supply chains into integrated value systems*. Upper Saddle River, NJ: Financial Times Prentice Hall.

Hugos, M. (2006). *Essentials of supply chain management* (2nd ed.). Hoboken, NJ: John Wiley & Sons, Inc.

Kuglin, F., & Hook, J. (2002). *Building, leading, and managing strategic alliances: How to work effectively and profitably with partner companies*. New York, NY: American Management Association.

Li, Suhong, Ragu-Nathan, B., Ragu-Nathan, T. S., & Subba Rao, S. (2006). The impact of supply chain management practices on competitive advantage and organizational performance. *Omega, 34*(2), 107-124.

Mitchell, D., Coles, C., Golisano, B. T., & Knutson, R. B. (2003). *The ultimate competitive advantage: Secrets of continually developing a more profitable business model*. San Francisco, CA: Berrett-Koehler Publishers.

Segil, L. (2002). *Intelligent business alliances: How to profit using today's most important strategic tool*. New York, NY: Three Rivers Press.

Segil, L. D. (2004). *Measuring the value of partnering: How to use metrics to plan, develop, and implement successful alliances*. New York, NY: American Management Association.

Simchi-Levi, D., Kaminsky, P., & Simchi-Levi, E. (2003). *Managing the supply chain: The definitive guide for the business professional*. New York, NY: McGraw-Hill.

Talluri, S., Baker, R. C., & Sarkis, J. (1999). A framework for designing efficient value chain networks. *International Journal of Production Economics, 62*(1/2), 133-144.

Wallace, R. (2004). *Strategic partnerships: An entrepreneur's guide to joint ventures and alliances*. Chicago, IL: Kaplan Business.

CLUSTER Q: RUNNING A PROFITABLE BUSINESS

Never be frightened to take a profit. Better in your pocket then theirs.
Michael Levy – Author and poet

*The most important single central fact about a free market
is that no exchange takes place unless both parties benefit.*
Milton Friedman – Economist and Nobel Prize winner

THE SIGNPOST

No question here, right? You need profit if you want to stay in business. It's the ultimate business scorecard. Profit in pure accounting terms is one thing, true economic profit is another. Organizations that create true wealth consistently, that deliver financial results year in and year out are a rare breed. They have learned how to provide value to every stakeholder, to correct weaknesses in every business function, and to execute a sound business plan with precision. They're worth emulating.

ITEMS

17. Improve profitability and business results every year
37. Have high productivity; use resources efficiently
57. Have predictable financial results

UNSKILLED

- Makes poor strategic decisions
- Hires and develops talent ineffectively
- Ignores customers; doesn't listen
- Fails to closely monitor the competition
- Doesn't understand costs or aggressively work to reduce costs
- Doesn't allocate capital wisely or choose the best sources of capital
- Sets prices inappropriately; misses sales or leaves money on the table
- Doesn't execute well; lacks follow-through
- Doesn't respond to marketplace changes
- Fails to innovate effectively

SKILLED

- Is intimate with customers; thoroughly understands their needs
- Establishes and communicates goals that are crystal clear
- Organizes the business so it most effectively provides value to the customer
- Designs effective processes and never stops improving

- Hires and develops the very best talent
- Relentlessly drives costs and inefficiencies out of the business
- Sets prices to optimize long-term return to the organization
- Invests wisely in innovation
- Aggressively works to build brand loyalty
- Applies understanding of the cost of capital to make sound financial decisions
- Understands the role of intangibles in building value
- Embeds measurement into business processes

SOME CAUSES

- Lacks business acumen
- Doesn't understand or anticipate customer needs
- Lacks action orientation; not proactive
- Doesn't prioritize
- Lacks perspective
- Ignores details
- Ineffective planning
- Poor strategic decisions
- Lack of financial discipline

THE TEN LEADERSHIP ARCHITECT® COMPETENCIES MOST ASSOCIATED WITH THIS CLUSTER (in order of connectedness)

35. Managing and Measuring Work
50. Priority Setting
53. Drive for Results
 5. Business Acumen
52. Process Management
63. Total Work Systems (e.g., TQM/ISO/Six Sigma)
15. Customer Focus
39. Organizing
47. Planning
51. Problem Solving

THE MAP

Profit is good. Profitable, healthy businesses begin with the customer. A for-profit business supplies a product or service for which the customer is willing to pay a margin over and above the cost of supplying that good or service. That difference, basically what's left after you subtract expenses from revenue, is called profit. This explanation borders on oversimplification, but it's clear to anyone that businesses must create a profit. Without profit, it's only a matter of time before a business folds. Profit is used to grease the wheels of the business so it can continue to operate and grow and to reward investors in the enterprise. Profit funds innovation, attracts talent to the organization, attracts investors (thus decreasing the cost of capital), and attracts customers to the extent they want to do business with a company that is on solid footing and stable. Basically, there are only two ways a business can increase profit: grow top-line sales or increase the profit margin, the relationship between revenue and expenses. Margin is improved when prices are raised or when operating expenses are reduced. Astute businesspeople understand that cost reduction has a larger impact and more certain result on margins than an increase in price. Businesses that have long-term, predictable profitability do most things well. They continually reinvent themselves in response to customer needs. They operate with the leanest possible assets. They relentlessly look for and seize opportunities to drive costs out of the business without sacrificing quality and service. They understand the cost of capital and employ capital wisely. They generate profit. And profit is good.

SOME REMEDIES

1. **Plan strategically.** Long-term business health requires strategy, and strategy starts with the customer. What do customers need? Want? What are they willing to pay for? Where are they? How do they want the product or service delivered? Who (besides you) do they want to buy from? What's the history of your products and services in your industry? Where are the raw materials? Who controls the market? What breakthrough strategy (if executed; and that's a big if) would work best? What have others tried? What are your competitors most likely to do? Strategy is a known field. Michael Porter's series of books is probably the best place to start if strategy is an issue. There are also many fine strategy consultants in the marketplace if you need help. Get your strategy right before anything else. Put it all together in a business plan. Your business plan is your roadmap for achieving long-term, sustainable, predictable profitability. It identifies your customers and describes what and how you provide value for them. Your plan will lay out your profit model, describe your business processes that deliver value to the customer, present financial information—projections, budgets, sources and costs of capital, use of assets, pricing, etc.—and describe your strategy for building customer loyalty. Write it clearly so that it can be used as a communication vehicle with your investors and employees.

2. **Learn about profit models.** Start with the macro. Study Adrian Slywotzky's *The Art of Profitability*. Analyze the profit models and hold them up against your business. Do this for each of your competitors to compare and contrast models. Go outside your industry and study the profit models of best-in-class companies in a variety of industries. Will any of those models work for your business? Play out scenarios to determine what would happen to the business landscape if one or more of your key competitors changed to a new profit model.

117

3. **Build the business acumen from the top down.** What's the financial literacy level in your organization? Turn business leaders into teachers and coaches to provide others with the basics—reading income statements, balance sheets, and statements of cash flow. Leaders in finance should teach the ratios and metrics they use to measure business performance. Promote financial literacy so employees are conversant with the terms used in finance. Distribute annual reports for study, including those of Berkshire Hathaway and the accompanying letters to shareholders from the chairman, Warren Buffett. These are available for download from www.berkshirehathaway.com. Have leaders read the *Wall Street Journal* and other business publications such as *Forbes*, *BusinessWeek*, and *Fortune*.

4. **Understand the cost of capital.** Encourage all leaders to learn about sources of capital and their associated costs. Have them study Economic Value Added (EVA) to learn the difference between accounting profit and economic profit. There is considerable information available from Stern Stewart & Co. at their Web site: www.sternstewart.com. Carefully analyze your business through the EVA lens. Teach the time-value of money and how to use net present value calculations in making investment decisions. A good source of information is in the articles available at www.investopedia.com. Apply financial learnings to budgeting at all levels throughout the organization.

5. **Focus on costs.** Cost reduction is the single most important lever to improve profit. A dollar in cost reduction has far more impact on profit than an extra dollar of sales revenue. Study the costs in your business. Dig into each expense line in your income statement to learn what makes up the number. Identify where the costs occur in your business processes and then work on your processes to remove costs. Pay particular attention to overhead and to fixed costs. Apply discipline from continuous improvement disciplines (Six Sigma, TQM, business process reengineering, etc.) to help study and manage costs.

6. **Focus on assets.** Analyze your assets. Consider your tangible assets—property, facilities, equipment, inventory, and receivables—and calculate what all these assets are costing your business. Have managers work with finance professionals to analyze opportunities for leasing assets rather than purchasing. Depending on terms, leasing may result in lower income but higher EVA. Choose EVA. Look for ways to delay capital investments and extend the life of assets. Optimize your inventory and streamline production processes to reduce work-in-progress. Consider your receivables and how reducing receivables impacts EVA. There are no shortages of opportunities to improve the wealth-creating power of your business. Line managers should build relations with their colleagues in finance and seek opportunities to learn from them.

7. **Focus on quality of sales.** Increasing your top line is good, but increasing the quality of sales is even better. How do your net sales compare with total revenue? To what extent are you losing profit to adjustments, discounts, warranty claims, and returned goods? Reducing these items is usually easier than boosting sales and is much more lucrative. Educate line employees on the costs associated with these elements. The great thing here is that these improvements not only drop right to the bottom line to directly impact profitability, they also indirectly add to long-term profit by increasing customer satisfaction and loyalty. Tirelessly improve quality and delivery to reduce the difference between total revenue and net sales.

8. **Innovate.** Don't sacrifice long-term profitability and stability for short-term profits gained by skimping on research and development. Prudent investments in innovation are the way you can lay claim to future profitability. Apply the same management discipline you use with other business processes to your R&D function. Provide clear focus so every project is targeted on a market that has customers who will pay for the fruits of your efforts. Develop your R&D managers. In addition to technical expertise, they need strong project management skills and business acumen. R&D needs budgets, deliverables, and deadlines just as much as sales and production groups. After you've developed functional excellence in R&D, lead your organization in embracing innovation at all levels. Solicit and reward ideas from all quarters. Develop a formalized decision process for selecting R&D projects and teach the simplified version to all employees so they appreciate the discipline and generate better ideas. You'll get ideas that come out of left field and require unplanned investments. As much as possible, adopt them if they provide quick wins. Communicate and celebrate these wins to build a culture of innovation in your organization.

9. **Price effectively.** Prices form another profit lever and should be strategically determined as part of your marketing efforts. Raising prices, even a small amount, can have a huge impact on profitability. The impact of price increases, though, is often unpredictable and fails to follow the tidy economic curves you learned in Econ 101 to describe supply and demand and price elasticity. If only things were so simple. The reality is that customers often act irrationally. So, how do you set prices? The most common mistake is to assume that your costs form the basis of prices. You do have to know your costs and consider them, but they do more to establish the pricing floor than to lead you to an optimum price. Another common mistake is to follow the pricing of competitors. Again, knowing your competitors prices is important, but it shouldn't be the sole basis of your pricing decision unless you think your competitors are a whole lot smarter than you. Study different pricing models: differential pricing, value pricing, product line pricing, promotional pricing, geographical pricing, premium pricing, etc. Tap into

marketing expertise and knowledge of your customer base to carefully consider how packaging, positioning, branding, and discounts should be implemented. The key is to consider pricing to be a strategic marketing decision, not simply a financial decision.

10. **Create customer loyalty.** Since your goal is to create long-term profitability and predictability, it's essential to focus on building customer loyalty. The strength of your brand is an intangible asset that leads to tangible results in the form of returning profitable business. A brand is a promise to the customer, and the strength of the brand is a direct reflection of the trust the customer places in your product. It's all about knowing what the customer wants, avoiding raising false expectations, and then never, ever underdelivering. The result of the first transaction is that customers are delighted—you'll have certainly met and likely exceeded their expectations—the first step in building the trust is taken. If you consistently deliver what customers want, if you consistently deliver what you promise, the trust—customer loyalty and brand value—increases with each transaction. So, what are the keys? Know what the customer wants. Put systems in place so that at every customer touch point you've assured that expectations will be met or exceeded. Never lose sight of the customer touch points. Measure them. Hold people accountable for keeping commitments, especially to customers. Remember that one botched transaction can undo years of hard work spent building customer loyalty. Consider investing in a customer relationship management (CRM) system. As in all other aspects of business, it's probably true that a small number of your customers (usually 20%) deliver the majority of your real profit (usually 80%). Do you know who they are? Many business theorists and consultants argue for trimming your customers down to the profitable ones. What would your profits be if you had an organization that was sized and designed to serve the needs of just your best customers? What if you fired your most troublesome customers? We all have them. They cause lots of noise, take up a lot of time. They might not be worth the trouble. Look to see if taking a systematic view of getting rid of noisy and time-consuming customers would result in a better business.

11. **Measure.** You can't manage without measurement. Starting with your highest level strategic objectives, break these down into actionable goals that address each of the four quadrants of a balanced scorecard: financial metrics, measures of customer satisfaction, indicators of employee engagement and learning, and finally, measures of your processes and innovation. Look for opportunities to measure quality, productivity, timeliness, and cost in each quadrant. Write your goals to reflect the elements of the commonly used SMART acronym—they should be specific, measurable, achievable (but aggressive), results-focused, and time-bound. Look for ways to measure inputs, processes, outputs, and outcomes. For example, measuring the quality of incoming raw materials is an input metric;

measuring cycle time gives you information about the productivity of a process; timeliness of employee on-boarding activities is an output metric of your talent management process; and your quarterly financial results are key outcomes. Finally, make your measures visible in your organization, speak about them at every opportunity, and provide feedback and reinforcement to those who work to achieve your organization's goals.

12. **Execute.** Jack Welch, former chairman of General Electric, put it this way: "Follow through on everything. Follow-up is one key measure of success of a business. Your follow-up business strategy will pave the way for your success." You can read the details of how this has been achieved at GE and Honeywell by reading *Execution* by Larry Bossidy and Ram Charan. There is simply no substitute for execution. All the brilliant ideas and planning in the world won't make a difference if the hard work of execution isn't done. And this is, indeed, the hard work of management. Simple, but hard. It takes discipline, focus, attention to details, and commitment to promises you've made to you customers, your investors, and your employees. Hold yourself and others accountable.

SUGGESTED READINGS

Barney, J. (1991). Firm resources and sustained competitive advantage. *Journal of Management, 17*(1), 99-120.

Bossidy, L., & Charan, R. (2002). *Execution: The discipline of getting things done.* New York, NY: Random House.

Bossidy, L., & Charan, R. (2004). *Confronting reality: Doing what matters to get things right.* New York, NY: Random House.

Callahan, K. (2005). *The management playbook: A step-by-step guide to accelerating the growth and profitability of your business.* Portland, OR: Inkwater Press.

Christensen, C. M., Roth, E. A., & Anthony, S. D. (2004). *Seeing what's next: Using theories of innovation to predict industry change.* Boston, MA: Harvard Business School Press.

Click, R. L., & Duening, T. N. (2004). *Business process outsourcing: The competitive advantage.* Hoboken, NJ: John Wiley & Sons.

Collis, D. J., & Cynthia, A. M. (1995 July/August). Competing on resource strategy in the 1990s. *Harvard Business Review, 73*(4), 118-128.

Collis, D. J., & Cynthia, A. M. (1998). *Corporate strategy: A resource-based view.* Boston, MA: Irwin/McGraw-Hill.

Daly, J. L. (2001). *Pricing for profitability: Activity-based pricing for competitive advantage.* New York, NY: John Wiley & Sons, Inc.

Grant, R. M. (1991). The resource-based theory of competitive advantage: Implications for strategy formulation. *California Management Review, 33*(3), 114-135.

Kaplan, R. S., & Cooper, R. (1997). *Cost & effect: Using integrated cost systems to drive profitability and performance.* Boston, MA: Harvard Business School Press.

Reichheld, F. (2006). *The ultimate question: Driving good profits and true growth.* Boston, MA: Harvard Business School Press.

Simon, H., Bilstein, F., & Luby, F. (2006). *Manage for profit, not for market share: A guide to greater profits in highly contested markets.* Boston, MA: Harvard Business School Press.

Slater, R. (2002). *29 Leadership secrets from Jack Welch.* New York, NY: McGraw-Hill.

Slywotzky, A. (2003). *The art of profitability.* New York, NY: Warner Business Books.

Slywotzky, A., Morrison, D., & Andelman, B. (2002). *The profit zone: How strategic business design will lead you to tomorrow's profits.* New York, NY: Three Rivers Press.

Welch, J., & Byrne, J. (2001). *Jack: Straight from the gut.* New York, NY: Warner Business Books.

Welch, J., & Welch, S. (2005). *Winning.* New York, NY: HarperCollins.

*A market is never saturated with a good product,
but it is very quickly saturated with a bad one.*
Henry Ford – Founder, Ford Motor Company

*When I am working on a problem, I never think about beauty,
I think only of how to solve the problem. But when I have finished,
if the solution is not beautiful, I know it is wrong.*
Richard Buckminster Fuller – Architect, inventor, poet, and author

THE SIGNPOST

Beauty is in the eye of the beholder. So is value. What do your customers value? Your investors? Employees? What is your value proposition? You've got to define it, communicate it, and deliver on it. Do it well. Do it consistently. Never stop.

ITEMS

18. Deliver value to our investors and other relevant shareholders
38. Deliver value to our customers
58. Deliver value (workplace, job, career) to our employees
76. Deliver value to the communities in which we operate

UNSKILLED

- Is inwardly focused; doesn't pay attention to all stakeholders
- Oversells, overpromises, and underdelivers value
- Uses the wrong metrics to drive performance
- Fails to listen
- Is inattentive to details, sloppy in execution
- Is complacent; makes decisions slowly
- Lacks customer sensitivity and focus
- Fails to deliver on key investor expectations
- Doesn't give back to the community more than required
- Fails to invest in and engage employees

SKILLED

- Has broad perspective and considers needs of all stakeholders
- Seeks input, listens closely, accepts all feedback, and responds with action
- Prudently sets expectations and communicates openly and honestly

- Establishes a culture infused with cooperation, trust, inclusion, and passion for the strategy
- Consistently and flawlessly executes to deliver on commitments
- Establishes meaningful goals in a balanced scorecard and metrics to track performance
- Fully integrates the organization into local community life
- Organizes business processes to best meet customer needs
- Delivers predictable, superior financial performance
- Demonstrates civic pride, good global citizenship

SOME CAUSES

- Narrow perspective
- Doesn't invest wisely
- Limited strategy and vision
- Internally focused; diverted by self-interests
- Defensive to constituency criticism
- Financially unsophisticated
- Doesn't buy into social and community responsibility
- Only adopts routine financial metrics

THE TEN LEADERSHIP ARCHITECT® COMPETENCIES MOST ASSOCIATED WITH THIS CLUSTER (in order of connectedness)

15. Customer Focus

33. Listening

53. Drive for Results

51. Problem Solving

58. Strategic Agility

5. Business Acumen

46. Perspective

50. Priority Setting

28. Innovation Management

65. Managing Vision and Purpose

THE MAP

Providing value to all stakeholders is the winning strategy. Value is always defined through the eyes of the receiver, so value depends upon the constituency. For customers, it's products and services they want, delivered conveniently, and priced reasonably. The revenue returned to the organization fuels operations, investments in innovation, and, if the business is operating effectively, returns dividends to the investors. Win-win. In exchange for predictable return on their capital, investors continue to provide capital. Win-win. Employees value interesting and challenging work, opportunities for growth and development, pride in accomplishments, camaraderie with coworkers, and equitable financial compensation for their contributions. In return, they come to work fully engaged every day, passionate about achieving the organization's goals, and committed to the values and mission. Win-win. Communities value organizations that provide good jobs for citizens and take their civic responsibilities seriously by contributing more than is required for the well-being of the community. In exchange, they provide infrastructure and an environment that supports the organization's operations and attracts talent to the area. Win-win. Consider all stakeholders when shaping the mission and vision of the organization. Set goals in a balanced scorecard that includes your various constituencies. It's good for business.

SOME REMEDIES

1. **Determine your value proposition.** For each stakeholder, define your value proposition. Begin by identifying the various constituencies. Describe in some detail what they want from your organization. Be aggressive. Listen closely. Study carefully. Learn about their expectations. Listen to the voice of the customer. Use a variety of methods—market research, focus groups, trend analysis, surveys, etc. Listen to your employees. Talk to them. Utilize engagement and climate surveys. Listen to shareholders. Talk to key investors. Get to know them. Get to know other key stakeholders. Meet with community representatives, regulators, legislators, suppliers, alliance partners, etc. Couch everything in a business context and address deliverables and expectations. Now quantify the value you receive from each of the stakeholders. Is every relationship win-win? Likely not. You may learn that you need to significantly enhance your deliverables for a constituency if you want to maintain the relationship. You may learn that you simply can't reasonably meet the expectations of a stakeholder. Or, you may choose not to because doing so violates your values or strategic intent. At least you'll know. You may turn away some investors, some customers, or partners. Some business isn't worth the effort. Some business presents ethical dilemmas that aren't worth potentially troublesome consequences. Some stakeholders are too difficult to work with. Getting clear about your value proposition related to all stakeholders will shape your approach to business and define your real currency of success.

2. **Cement your value proposition in the strategy.** Include elements of your value proposition in the collateral of your organization. Aside from stand-alone statements, embed it in your strategy, your vision and mission statements, and in your business objectives. Include value propositions in your annual report. Put them in recruiting brochures and your advertising. Include them in employee orientation. Make them part of the fabric of your organization.

3. **Deliver your value proposition.** Establish realistic, and aligned, expectations. Don't make promises that you can't keep to impress stakeholders, to snare a new constituency. Avoid the temptation to set lofty goals and targets that you're not capable of achieving. It's great to stretch to meet goals. It's fantastic to exceed them. But it's no fun to miss them, to have to explain and justify to investors or customers why you failed to make your commitment. The fallout can be swift and severe—disillusionment and abandonment. Earn the trust of your stakeholders. Underpromise and consistently overdeliver.

4. **Deliver financial value.** Focus on the most appropriate financial metrics to drive your business. In addition to typical revenue and income metrics, measure economic value added (EVA) or a variation to assess your organization's true wealth-creating performance. Drive financial and business training deeply and broadly into the organization so that all managers and leaders are sophisticated and can make good financial decisions. Make sure that managers can readily measure, interpret, and explain the financial performance of their respective business units against your established metrics. Hold them accountable for doing so. Work to drive down costs. Cost reduction is the single most important lever to improve profit. A dollar in cost reduction has far more impact on profit than an extra dollar of sales revenue. Study the costs in your business. Dig into each expense line in your income statement to learn what makes up the number. Identify where the costs occur in your business processes and then work on your processes to remove costs. Pay particular attention to overhead and to fixed costs. Apply discipline from continuous improvement disciplines (Six Sigma, TQM, business process reengineering, etc.) to help study and manage costs. Analyze your assets. Consider your tangible assets—property, facilities, equipment, inventory, and receivables—and calculate what all these assets are costing your business. Look for ways to delay capital investments and extend the life of assets. Optimize your inventory and streamline production processes to reduce work-in-progress. Consider your receivables and how reducing receivables impacts EVA. Work to improve the quality of your sales, to minimize adjustments, discounts, warranty claims, and returned goods. Reducing these items is usually easier than boosting sales and is much more lucrative. Educate line employees on the costs associated with these elements. The great thing here is that these improvements not only drop right to the bottom line to directly impact profitability, they also indirectly add to long-term profit by increasing customer satisfaction and loyalty.

Tirelessly improve quality and delivery to reduce the difference between total revenue and net sales. There are no shortages of opportunities to improve the wealth-creating power of your business.

5. **Deliver value to your customers.** Create a strong marketing and sales promotion function. Staff it with the best talent you can find and afford. Understand your customers and your competition. Constantly run client surveys to keep abreast of what they find valuable. What do they want, need, and expect of you? Talk to key customers. Have customers come in and work with employees on new products and services. Do the same for a wide range of prospective customers. Ask about both tangibles and intangibles. Vary these surveys by region or country to enable you to get to granular differences. Differentiate your customers in terms of their value to you and pay significantly more attention to the ones further up the food chain. Also, keep a steady eye on current and emerging competition. Compare yourself to best in the world. Look beyond your industry or organizations normally thought of as competitors. Look to best-in-class competitors, regardless of industry. Consider other types of businesses and other parts of the world. Pay special attention to the fringe, including small, innovative companies. Study customer trends.

6. **Deliver value to employees.** Keep track of the collective employee pulse. Conduct frequent employee satisfaction and engagement surveys to be able to fully understand what your employees value. Measure both absolute levels of engagement and your progress from period to period. Follow up in a meaningful way with all identified needs, in a prioritized order. Get people involved in the design and implementation of solutions so they own the approaches and solutions. The goal for most organizations is to be the preferred employer or the employer of choice for the specific kinds of talent the organization needs to fulfill its mission. Several business publications and professional organizations publish a list each year of preferred employers and the best places to work. Study the evaluation criteria used by those lists to learn how those firms attract, engage, and retain talent. In general, employees want to get along with their coworkers, feel they're being fairly compensated, and have a sense of pride in their work accomplishments. In exchange for those benefits, they will be loyal, productive, and stay with the organization. At a more granular level, you may find that employees vary in terms of what they want from the job based on certain categories—for example, job families, demographic groups, job position levels, geographic location, etc. Some employees value flexible time more than others. Some put more value on office space and furnishings than others. Learn what's important and treat people as they want to be treated. Pay particular attention to your key talent. Use a wide variety of levers to engage employees. Start with the overall pay and benefits package, and then build on it to create a total rewards

R: CREATING VALUE

DIMENSION VI: MANAGING PROFITABILITY AND DELIVERING VALUE

strategy that gives you a competitive edge over the competition in attracting and retaining the best talent. Invest in employees' development. Design career paths and options that employees perceive as valuable and contribute to their engagement. Make sure to develop the interpersonal skills in your managers that will result in better employee-boss relationships and contribute to employee retention.

7. **Deliver value to the community.** Become pillars of local communities where you have significant operations. Join forces with community leaders to learn what's important to them, where the enterprise can be of most assistance. Get employees involved on the boards of community not-for-profit organizations. Make it corporate policy to have volunteer days where groups of employees work together doing meaningful, tangible projects in local neighborhoods. Align with good causes. Contribute funds for a local landmark or charity that adds value to the community and helps build your brand. When possible, open up company facilities for community programs and activities. Set up community partnerships to achieve visible goals. Be environmentally and socially responsible. Institutionalize a social responsibility function. Reduce energy. Develop green technology. Evolve your value proposition from one that benefits only direct customers, shareholders, and employees to one that has long-term benefits for the larger world. Target a meaningful cause that's aligned with your values, contributes to your branding, and does something significantly good for the world. Be the best in the world and be the best for the world.

8. **Add value through innovation.** A lot of incremental value comes from innovation. Become known for innovation. Constantly come out with a variety of new offerings every season. Play around the fringe. Refresh your core products or services. Strategically select the attributes on which you want to compete and aggressively work to deliver on those values. Focus on developing new innovations that have long coattails, innovations that provide opportunities for numerous enhancements and variations that add value. Grow new markets by tailoring products and services to differentiated target customers. Create customer experiences that go beyond just delivering at a high level to making the interaction memorable. Reward people for taking risks to be innovative. Reward valiant attempts that end in failure. Inspire and challenge.

9. **Communicate your value proposition.** Consider your stakeholders and create targeted messages for each constituency that clearly communicates your value proposition and builds your brand. Engage an internal or external PR staff to help create key messages. Establish context around the message. Use multiple methods to communicate. Employ new communication technologies effectively. Create an employee Web site. Create videos. Schedule information lunches. Create a newsletter. Create special forums to share. Build internal communications

channels. Make sure employees find out your value proposition and how you're delivering value to all stakeholders.

10. **Celebrate value.** Embed value creation in your culture. Tell the stories of employees who have conquered challenges to deliver value for stakeholders. Create legends of value creation. Celebrate great accomplishments with awards and ceremonies. Reward the behaviors that lead to value. Publish stories in company newsletters and on your intranet site. Make the stories part of executive speeches. Build the legacy of providing value.

SUGGESTED READINGS

Cohen, B., & Warwick, M. (2006). *Value-driven business: How to change the world, make money, and have fun.* San Francisco, CA: Berret-Koehler Publishers.

DeBonis, J. N., Balinski, E. W., & Allen, P. (2002). *Value-based marketing for bottom line success: 5 Steps to creating customer value.* New York, NY: McGraw-Hill.

Fombrum, C. J., Van Riel, C. (2003). *Fame and fortune: How successful companies build winning reputations.* Upper Saddle River, NJ: Financial Times Prentice Hall.

Kouses, J. M., & Posner, B. Z. (2006). *A leader's legacy.* San Francisco, CA: Jossey-Bass.

Lawler, E., III, & Lawler, E. E. (2003). *Treat people right: How organizations and employees can create a win/win relationship to achieve high performance at all levels.* San Francisco, CA: Jossey-Bass.

Pfeffer, J. (2005). Producing sustainable competitive advantage through the effective management of people. *Academy of Management Executive, 19*(4), 95-106.

Pine, J. B., & Gilmore, J. H. (1999). *Experience economy: Work is theater and every business a stage.* Boston, MA: Harvard Business School Press.

Rappaport, A. (1997). *Creating shareholder value: A guide for managers and investors.* New York, NY: Free Press.

Savitz, A., & Weber, K. (2006). *The triple bottom line: How today's best-run companies are achieving economic, social and environmental success—and how you can too.* San Francisco, CA: Jossey-Bass.

Thakor, A. Y. (2000). *Becoming a better value creator: How to improve the company's bottom line—and your own.* San Francisco, CA: Jossey-Bass.

Ulrich, D., & Brockbank, W. (2005). *The HR value proposition.* Boston, MA: Harvard Business School Press.

Weinzimer, P. (1998). *Getting it right! Creating customer value for market leadership*. New York, NY: John Wiley & Sons.

CLUSTER S: FILLING THE TALENT BENCH

My main job was developing talent. I was a gardener
providing water and other nourishment to our top 750 people.
Of course, I had to pull out some weeds, too.
Jack Welch – Former Chairman and CEO, General Electric

You look for stars. You look for the makeup of artists
who can have long lasting careers and who could be headliners.
Clive Davis – Founder, Arista Records, and record producer

THE SIGNPOST

What does your talent pipeline look like? How do you fill it? How do you identify high-potential candidates, the ones with the potential to fill senior leadership positions in your organization? Do you assess potential as well as performance? How do you assess learning agility? How do you develop it? What is your build-versus-buy strategy for talent? You need to have ready answers to these questions to have any chance at beating your competition in the war for talent.

ITEMS

19. Have a well-supported process in place to identify and develop the next generation of leaders
39. Move people across functional, geographic, and business unit boundaries for development as future leaders
59. Accurately differentiate our people based on potential (high, moderate, low)
77. Accurately distinguish between our top, middle, and bottom performers
89. Have senior management and/or the board actively engaged in our talent management process
94. Use job assignments to build new skills in high-potential employees
95. Acquire talent from outside as needed for key positions

UNSKILLED

- Fails to make talent management a priority
- Operates talent management without full engagement of top management and the board
- Doesn't use best practice talent management tools and processes
- Leaves business units and functions to manage talent on their own
- Lacks HR stewardship and credibility
- Makes inaccurate and inflated calls on performance and potential

- Fails to effectively identify and assign jobs for development
- Allows line managers to interfere with moving people across business units for development
- Fails to create a feedback-rich culture
- Leaves individuals to manage their own development
- Fails to achieve appropriate ratio of internal promotions to new hires from outside
- Doesn't provide rewards or incentives to managers who are the best people developers

SKILLED

- Views talent as fundamental to the achievement of enterprise goals
- Uses best practices succession management tools and processes
- Links executive and management incentives/compensation to talent goals
- Manages high-potential talent centrally for the entire enterprise
- Is fully engaged in talent management at the top management and board levels
- Has alignment and support at all levels to promote talent deployment for development
- Fills most senior jobs from inside with successful candidates
- Recruits some external high-potential candidates to ensure new perspectives and diversity
- Effectively assesses skills provided by jobs; uses information for development assignments
- Doesn't shy away from making tough calls related to performance and potential
- Builds a culture that promotes frequent, honest, and actionable feedback
- Provides ample development opportunities through jobs, training, coaching, and mentoring

SOME CAUSES

- Confusion about the talent proposition
- Culture struggles with differential treatment
- Avoids making tough calls and associated conflict
- Insufficient investment in talent
- Narrow perspective; short-term view
- Afraid to give tough feedback
- Senior management not engaged in talent process
- Talent management not centralized
- HR function not credible with senior management
- Expectations for training results unrealistic
- Internal resistance to moving people for development
- Inaccurate people assessments
- No shared mind-set on talent

THE TEN LEADERSHIP ARCHITECT® COMPETENCIES MOST
ASSOCIATED WITH THIS CLUSTER (in order of connectedness)

56. Sizing Up People

12. Conflict Management

58. Strategic Agility

2. Dealing with Ambiguity

46. Perspective

13. Confronting Direct Reports

52. Process Management

36. Motivating Others

47. Planning

19. Developing Direct Reports and Others

THE MAP

It's still all about talent. Always has been and will be in the future. People of talent achieve great things. Teams of talent win. Enterprises full of talent win. The next war for talent is upon us as the baby boomers around the world move into retirement. This is going to be much worse than the first talent war in the 1990s. Fifty percent of the people on the management committees of America's largest companies will be gone by 2012. CEO tenure is down to a median of five years in the U.S. and seven years internationally. Replacement pools are weak, and outside talent is hard to find. There is a greater demand for talent than there is supply. Corporate boards of directors and the investment community view talent as a risk factor they must monitor on an ongoing basis. So, having the talent to run the business has become a nearly universal top priority for most organizations. Companies that have effective build-and-buy talent strategies are going to be the only ones able to compete successfully. The research is in. Best practices are known. Success stories abound. Results and ROI have been documented. So really, all that's left is execution. Organizations that miss the flight will not get to their destinations.

SOME REMEDIES

1. **Engage top management.** Nothing happens until you have top management support. All the studies on effective talent management organizations note the commitment and involvement of top management. Start by projecting the human capital requirements to implement the organization's competitive strategies. Set aggressive goals that will push your talent management practices ahead of your competition. Implement workforce planning to understand the critical jobs and the internal and external resource pools available to fill them. Inform key decision makers about the projected shortage of workers in all job categories to

DIMENSION VII: DEVELOPING FUTURE LEADERS

S: TALENT BENCH

133

ensure that adequate attention and resources are devoted to talent attraction, development, and retention programs. Tie talent management excellence to the bottom line. Show top management the research on the connection between best practices in talent management and financial outcomes. If necessary, send top managers out to visit noncompetitive organizations that have implemented best practice talent management processes. Study and learn from the companies known for their talent processes, the places where top management—including the CEO and the rest of the executive committee—spends 30% to 40% of their time on people issues. Get top management in your organization actively involved in mentoring high potentials to help get the most learning possible from their experience. Extend this involvement up through the board of directors by having the board involved in key succession decisions and mentoring where appropriate. Bring in top talent management speakers. Buy books by Larry Bossidy and Jack Welch and distribute them to top management. Translate top management's intentions into the vision and mission statements. Insert talent management goals into the assessment process. Make it part of the strategy.

2. **Determine the mission-critical capabilities.** You need to know the destination before you can plan and execute the trip. You need to know what capabilities and skills are going to be necessary for the organization's future. You will first need to have some idea about the issues and challenges your organization will face at a specific time in the future, usually seven to ten years out. Ask questions like:

    - Where are the markets going to be for our products and services?

    - What is the corporate structure going to be? Centralized? Decentralized? By geographic zones? By product or service? What roles will be necessary for that structure?

    - What will our labor market look like? Composition of the labor pool? Percent out of home country? How severe will the talent shortage be?

    - Who will our customers be?

    - What governmental and regulatory issues will we face?

    - Who will our competitors be? What will they be doing?

    - How will business models evolve? How will world economies change?

    - What environmental issues will we be facing?

    - What will employees want and need from us?

    - What unions will we be working with?

    - What resources will we need to be competitive?

    - What will the political climate be like?

- What will our various stakeholders—shareholders, employees, customers, partners, governments, and communities—demand from us?

- What alliances will we need?

The answers to these questions will determine what capabilities and skills you will need in the future. These capabilities then become your targets for recruiting, performance management, and development.

3. **Determine the mission-critical experiences.** You need to know what types of experiences your people need, what they need to be exposed to in order to prepare them for future leadership. Using the answers to the same questions as listed in Number 2 above, determine what jobs will provide the best preparation for the future. You need to determine two different types of jobs. The first type of job is not industry- or market-specific—it's a general sort of job that builds focused business skills. These are jobs such as start-ups, fix-its, and international assignments. For the most part, these jobs will be found in the research done by the Center for Creative Leadership and outlined in the book *Lessons of Experience.* If you have done your own internal analysis, so much the better. People learn primarily from experience, and these jobs are the building blocks for certain key competencies and skills needed for future leaders. They can also fill the bill when there are expectations for key roles. They might even be unstated but common suppositions in your organization—for example, every CEO should have managed a start-up or had international experience. The second kind of job has particular relevance to your organization, your industry, or your markets. These jobs build skills that are especially appropriate for your business and can also meet key expectations for senior executive qualification—for example, all C-suite executives should have spent time in manufacturing, finance, and marketing, or all senior management should have had a job working with our dealership network. These jobs can be identified by considering the answers to the questions above. Of course, you can expect some overlap; there are some competencies addressed by both types of jobs. The key is to provide the right experiences and expose future leaders to a variety of situations that teach the competencies your organization needs to succeed in the future.

4. **Hire the best.** Talent management processes can't work if the right talent isn't in the pipeline. Nurture homegrown talent, but not exclusively. Fill about 20% of your top positions from the outside with high-talent people in order to avoid the type of insular thinking that comes from having a talent pool that is exclusively homegrown. Become particularly proficient at external recruiting and hiring. Learn to interview for talent. In addition to background, experience, and job skills, interview for competencies and potential. Use some system of structured interviewing. At senior levels, develop the capability of working well with executive recruiters to ensure that they send you the best talent. Always be on

the lookout for talent, even when you don't have open positions. Be a relentless talent scout so you have a ready supply waiting in the wings. Based upon your projections from the workforce planning studies, make sure the organization has sufficient talent throughout the organization.

5. **Assess potential talent more accurately.** Research has shown that typical line managers have difficulty making tough calls on potential. The most predictive indicator of potential is learning agility—adaptability, or the ability to learn from experience and develop rules of thumb that can subsequently be used to perform well in future first-time situations. Potential is not the same as performance. That's an erroneous connection most managers make, and it decreases the accuracy of the calls on potential. Many organizations have cultures that find high-potential identification distasteful; they feel it smacks of elitism and is akin to anointing someone from among the commoners as a prince or princess. It's not about labeling, it's about accurately finding your most talented people throughout the organization, and it requires honest assessment and tough calls. The characteristics of people with potential are well known, and there are assessment tools on the market to help managers make those calls.

6. **Provide actionable feedback**. Research is crystal clear—people need accurate, timely, and actionable feedback to grow and develop. In order to have best practice talent management, you must have a feedback-rich culture. People need to know where they stand. People need to know what they need to work on. People need to know their goals and targets. They need to know what the mission-critical competencies are, what the mission-critical jobs are. Put rigor into all feedback in your organization. Use ranking as well as rating in performance evaluations. Use 360° feedback. Use self-assessment. Urge all managers to be more critical in their feedback. Make feedback a daily task. Don't rely only on formal evaluation processes.

7. **Use a best practices talent review process.** Executing a top-notch people and talent review system takes commitment and work, but there are documented best practices to guide your organization. The elements of the system are agreed upon and well understood by experienced academics and practitioners. Audit your talent management system. Look to upgrade all of the elements to best practices. Look to publications from the Human Resource Planning Society and the Center for Creative Leadership for those best practices. See the references below.

8. **Use assignments to develop leaders.** Use a combination of on-the-job learning, guidance from people, and classroom learning to develop leaders in approximately the percentages outlined by the Center for Creative Leadership to be most effective. About 70% of development should come from full- and part-time job assignments. Give the most challenging jobs like start-ups and turnarounds to your high potentials. Aim to keep them in these jobs for about

136

33 months to ensure optimal learning. Assign skill coaches and provide the candid developmental feedback necessary to help people get the most from their jobs and to learn from any adversity they may encounter. Assign your mission-critical jobs (see above) to those you've identified as having the best potential.

9. **Provide development and differential treatment plans.** After assessing potential and identifying high-potential talent, you need action plans to ensure your talent is developed appropriately. There are many aspects to treatment but these are the main categories:

- **Compensation Plan:** What is the market value for talent? How much are high potentials worth to your organization? What would be the cost of replacing them? You have finite dollars to spend. What's the best way to distribute those dollars across all of the people? How much more should you pay a high-potential person than someone who is struggling?

- **Retention and Treatment Plan:** How hard would it be to replace someone from your high-potential talent pool? People stay with organizations for well-known reasons. Each talent classification represents a different value to the organization, and those with higher potential deserve more development and opportunities through treatment plans designed to prepare them, engage them, and retain them.

- **Development and Assignmentology Plan:** Research tells us that the prime source of development comes from on-the-job experience. Rich developmental jobs are scarce. Those jobs should be reserved for those who are best able to do them and will benefit most from them developmentally. Generally, the highest-talent people should get the first shot at developmentally rich jobs.

- **Exposure Plan:** There are mission-critical assignments that provide exposure to various business aspects essential for creating leadership capabilities for the future. Again, these may be assignments that rarely come available and should be given to those who can best do them and also benefit from them developmentally. Generally, the highest-talent people should get the first shot at developmentally rich jobs.

- **Engagement Plan:** People are different. They are motivated by different things. We want all employees to be engaged. Each talent classification requires a slightly different approach to engagement.

- **International Service Plan:** Global business is the norm, and a global perspective is probably mandatory for leaders in most organizations. International assignments are tough on people and families. But they are a necessary step to prepare for senior management roles. Consider your highest-talent people first for international assignments.

- **Assessment Plan:** Self-knowledge increases performance and aids development. Assessment costs money and takes time. There are different levels of assessment, depending upon talent classification. Choose the type and level of assessment most appropriate for your talent.

- **Mentoring Plan:** Mentors aid development, assimilation, and engagement. Running a mentoring program is time consuming and costly. Generally, the benefits will be limited to the higher-valued talent classifications.

- **Coaching Plan:** Everyone can benefit from a skills coach. With limited budgets and time, coaches are best employed in working with the higher-talent classifications.

- **Learning Agility Plan:** Learning agility is one of the key indicators of future potential. The ability to learn and gain from the experiences very significantly drives future performance. Research shows that learning agility can be enhanced in motivated people. Anyone can benefit from increasing learning agility, but time and budget limitations make it generally practical to focus efforts to develop learning agility in the higher talent classifications.

The simple point is to treat people differently based upon their potential and development needs.

10. **Institutionalize talent management metrics.** Use meaningful, results-based measurements that capture a variety of talent management effectiveness criteria. Track the numbers and percentages of key positions that are currently staffed with strong performers and also have qualified ready-now successors. Track numbers and percentages of executive positions filled with people from your internal talent pool. Track retention of key talent, the movement of high potentials between business units, the implementation and completion of robust development plans. Track targeted next-step development positions against actual fill rates. Measure the diversity levels in your high-potential pools and contrast with diversity in the organization at-large. Track year-to-year changes in diversity in the talent pools and executive ranks and follow the trends. Set goals against the metrics and hold top management accountable for achieving objectives. Meaningfully link management pay and promotability to the results. Incent managers for complying with and using the talent management system.

11. **Field a strong HR cadre.** Make sure that HR is fully capable of handling all aspects of the talent management process and has the needed credibility with line management to be sought out to provide guidance in talent decisions. The HR staff should have the strategic agility, perspective, and functional skills to design a succession program that is well suited to the organization. They should have the skills to execute and ensure the program's success, the perseverance to steward,

follow up, and continually improve the process without overcomplicating it. They need facilitation skills to lead talent discussions, the courage to be honest and direct, the intellectual horsepower and perspective to develop valuable personal opinions, and the widespread trust and respect of management.

SUGGESTED READINGS

Bennis, W., & Thomas, R. (2004). *Geeks and geezers.* Boston, MA: Harvard Business School Publishing.

Berke, D. (2005). *Succession planning and management.* Greensboro, NC: Center for Creative Leadership.

Byham, W. C., Smith, A. B., & Paese, M. J. (2002). *Grow you own leaders: How to identify, develop, and retain leadership talent.* Upper Saddle River, NJ: Financial Times Prentice Hall.

Byrne, J. C., & Rees, R. T. (2006). *The successful leadership development program: How to build it and how to keep it going.* San Francisco, CA: Pfeiffer.

Charan, R., Drotter, S., & Noel, J. (2001). *The leadership pipeline: How to build the leadership-powered company.* San Francisco, CA: Jossey-Bass.

Conger, J. A., & Fulmer, R. M. (2006, December). Developing your leadership pipeline. *Harvard Business Review, 81*(12), 76-84.

Corporate Leadership Council. (2004). *The leadership imperative strategy for increasing leadership bench strength.* Washington, DC: The Corporate Leadership Council.

Fulmer, R. M., & Conger, J. A. (2003). *Growing your company's leaders: How great organizations use succession management to sustain competitive advantage.* New York, NY: American Management Association.

Lombardo, M. M., & Eichinger, R. W. (2005). *The leadership machine* (3rd ed.). Minneapolis, MN: Lominger International: A Korn/Ferry Company.

McCall, M. W., Jr., Lombardo, M. M., & Morrison, A. M. (1988). *The lessons of experience: How successful executives develop on the job.* New York, NY: The Free Press.

Michaels, E., Handfied-Jones, H., & Axelrod, B. (2001). *The war for talent.* Boston, MA: Harvard Business School Press.

Munro, A. (2005). *Practical succession management: How to future-proof your organization.* Burlington, VT: Gower Publishing Company.

Rothwell, W. J. (2001). *Effective succession planning: Ensuring leadership continuity and building talent from within.* New York, NY: AMACOM.

Rothwell, W. J., Jackson, R. D., Knight, S. C., & Lindholm, J. E. (2005). *Career planning and succession management: Developing your organization's talent— For today and tomorrow*. Westport, CT: Praeger Publishers.

Cluster T: Managing in the Best Way

Too often it's not the most creative guys or the smartest. Instead,
it's the ones who are best at playing politics and soft-soaping their bosses.
Boards don't like tough, abrasive guys.
Carl Icahn – Investor and entrepreneur

You can't build a strong corporation with a lot of committees
and a board that has to be consulted every turn.
You have to be able to make decisions on your own.
Rupert Murdoch – Chairman, News Corporation

THE SIGNPOST

Rubber stamp boards are becoming a relic of the past, at least in public organizations. Pressures from investors and regulators are increasingly calling directors to task and holding them accountable for improprieties in the C-suite. But the best organizations don't just recruit watchdogs. They attract the best minds in business to the board and engage them in strategy development, talent development, and leveraging networks and resources.

ITEMS

20. Select and shape a board of directors that adds value
40. Actively engage the board of directors in the business
60. Effectively utilize outside resources (auditors, consultants, advisors, experts)
78. Manage the enterprise with appropriate transparency and openness

UNSKILLED

- Recruits directors for credentials and compliance, rather than strategic contribution
- Has board lacking managerial courage; strained relationship with CEO and top management
- Fails to clearly define roles and priorities
- Runs ineffective and inefficient meetings dominated by personalities
- Doesn't build a team or manage conflict effectively
- Fails to engage the board in succession and talent management
- Is unduly influenced by top management, the investment community, or other constituencies

- Lacks board skills and perspectives that complement and round out top management
- Limits board's direct access to the organization
- Is unnecessarily secretive and protective of information
- Focuses inwardly; doesn't leverage external expertise and networks; rejects consultants

SKILLED

- Aligns selection criteria for directors with strategic needs of the business
- Demonstrates integrity and independence; is not dominated by special interests
- Leverages board expertise, networks, and external resources to support top management
- Maintains productive working relationship between directors and top management
- Creates a climate of trust and teamwork; manages conflicts well
- Engages board in talent management, succession, and mentoring of key high potentials
- Promotes board independence, transparency, and accountability
- Is efficient in administration; runs productive meetings
- Provides ready access for board members to employees and relevant information
- Solicits feedback; listens well; is open to criticism; acts on information

SOME CAUSES

- Lack of strategic perspective
- Cronyism, nepotism
- Legacy bound
- Inwardly focused
- Defensiveness; aversion to criticism
- Lack of diversity and fresh perspectives
- External networks and resources not leveraged
- Lack of trust of key constituencies
- Unnecessary secrecy; inadequate information sharing

THE TEN LEADERSHIP ARCHITECT® COMPETENCIES MOST ASSOCIATED WITH THIS CLUSTER (in order of connectedness)

12. Conflict Management

27. Informing

46. Perspective

8. Comfort Around Higher Management

18. Delegation

33. Listening

DIMENSION VIII: GOVERNANCE

T: MANAGE THE BEST WAY

25. Hiring and Staffing

36. Motivating Others

52. Process Management

58. Strategic Agility

THE MAP

The world has changed. In the first three quarters of 2006, more than 21,000 C-level executives changed jobs, according to *Forbes* magazine. That's more than double the number from the previous year. About 1,200 CEOs left their office. Certainly, some of the pressure on senior executives is due to regulatory requirements that have increased the accountability of boards and spurred directors to proactively intervene more than they did before. The Sarbanes-Oxley Act of 2002, commonly called SOX or Sarbox, is a U.S. federal law designed to prevent scandals like those created by Enron, WorldCom, and others. It is designed to increase shareholder and investor confidence that the information they receive is correct. SOX established the Public Company Accounting Oversight Board to provide oversight and discipline of accounting firms that serve as auditors of public companies. SOX has substantially altered corporate governance in the U.S. by addressing issues such as auditor independence, financial disclosure, increased criminal and civil penalties for security law violations, and the protection of employees who blow the whistle on corporate fraud. The safeguards provided by SOX can cut both ways. One danger is that directors hunker down in a watchdog role, avoid risks, and limit their interventions to those contained in the letter of the law. Directors in effective organizations understand that SOX is there to provide a solid floor on which to establish their footing so they can reach for real accomplishments and meaningful contributions to the organization. Effective boards have their fingerprints everywhere: They hire the CEO, compensate the CEO, appraise the CEO, help plan succession for key positions, leverage their external networks to bring value to the business, actively partner with senior management to craft business strategy, speak up to provide counsel to the CEO, and step up in times of crisis to calm investors and the public. In the era of increased transparency, senior executives must deal with increased scrutiny and pressures from outside the enterprise. They have to be sensitive to many constituencies but not dominated by any one. Effective executives have to seek answers and solutions wherever they may be found. Increasingly, they're found outside the boundaries of the organization. They need to leverage partnerships with strategic alliance partners and external experts.

SOME REMEDIES

1. **Get the best board members – 1.** Your board is only as good as its directors. While it might be tempting to bring on a celebrity-status board member, you may be better off getting a hard-nosed, experienced business executive who's built a business or two, successfully turned around a failing business, and created real wealth. Thoroughly analyze and identify the competencies that will be most valuable to you in a board member, and then aggressively recruit the most-qualified people to fill your director positions. Do a future-back analysis. Pick a time in the future. You need to know the destination before you can plan and execute the trip. You need to know what capabilities and skills are going to be necessary for the organization's future. You will first need to have some idea about the issues and challenges your organization will face at a specific time in the future, usually seven to ten years out. Ask the current board and visionary internal resources to answer questions like the following:

- Who will our customers be?

- Where are the markets going to be for our products and services?

- What will the corporate structure look like? Centralized? Decentralized? Geographic zones? By product/service? What kinds of roles will be necessary for that structure?

- What will our labor market look like? People in short supply? Composition? Percent out of home country?

- What governmental and regulatory issues will we be facing?

- Who will our competitors be? What will they be doing?

- How will the business model evolve over time?

- What environmental issues will we be facing?

- What will employees want and need from us?

- What unions will we be working with?

- What resources will we need to be competitive?

- What will the political climate be like?

- What will our various stakeholders (shareholders, employees, customers, partners, governments, communities) demand from us?

- What alliances will we need?

The answers to these and similar questions will determine what competencies and skills you will need in the future. Look at these competencies and determine which ones will be adequately represented by members of top management. Which ones will be missing? The missing competencies will be useful as a guide for selecting multiple-term board members.

2. **Get the best board members – 2.** Determine the mission-critical experiences that will provide the perspectives necessary to make the best decisions at a specific time in the future. Use the same questions as above. You need to know what

kinds of background and experiences directors will need in order to provide top management with the best guidance. Use the answers to the questions listed above to determine those qualifications needed in the projected future. Consider international experience. What countries will comprise your dominant new markets over the next ten years? Get directors with direct experience and exposure to those markets. What resources will you need to be successful? Get directors with relevant experience. What business issues will be most critical? Mergers? Acquisitions? Strategic alliances? New products and services? Technology? Direct sales force? Regulatory issues? Legal issues? Union challenges? Immigration? Diversity? Manage the diversity of your board to reflect your future reality and emerging constituencies. It should be obvious that a company that sells products globally to various market segments should have a board composition that, to the extent possible, mirrors the global market and diverse customer base it serves. Look at the total list of the projected issues and challenges going forward and try to select board members with the background, experience, and skills that will best support and advise top management.

3. **Manage team dynamics.** The board is a team like any other team. All of the positive and negative things that go on in teams go on with boards. Egos. Conflict. Talkative and reticent team members. Disruptive members. Inattentive members. Members tardy or unprepared for meetings. Members leaving early. It's all normal for teams. The board chair has to run the team as the leader of any team. It's the chair's responsibility to define roles, set the agenda, facilitate the process, govern the members, and lead for effectiveness and success. There are typical team behaviors that get in the way of boards. There is off-line processing. In boards that are not well-run, too often significant business is transacted in smaller groups outside of formal meetings and processes. Cliques form and try to furtively assert influence on other directors. Obviously, this indicates a lack of trust and openness. Another issue is the undiscussable agenda. Undiscussables are things avoided in public. Research has shown that teams, including boards, are more effective when they don't allow topics to be out-of-bounds, when anything affecting the business is open for discussion. Another issue is talent deployment. This requires board members to step up and address the issues and challenges for which they are best suited. Board meetings can present another challenge that must be handled by the chair. Meetings should follow a process and ensure full participation of all, no dominance and no passivity by any member. As with all teams, there will be open and festering conflict. Chairs need to encourage constructive dissent and manage conflict so it's not damaging to the health of the team. So, simply, the board is a team like any other, and the principles of high-performing work teams need to be applied. It is usually a good practice for boards to set aside a meeting or two a year just for the purpose of team development, without an issue agenda, to learn to work together more effectively.

4. **Leverage external contacts and networks.** Experienced directors bring more than business acumen and background to the table. They bring a wealth of knowledge about other industries, contacts, and networks that can help build your business. Work with your directors to mine those contacts and networks to identify business opportunities. Use them as a source of recruiting, financial sources, ideas for mergers, acquisitions, and strategic alliances. Use them for regulatory and political leverage and access. You don't just select and engage the director as an individual, you get a network.

5. **Board access.** Don't let your board work in isolation. They should regularly rub shoulders with key employees. Use board members to grease your talent pipeline by assigning them to mentor key employees. Ask directors, as part of their responsibility, to be teachers and coaches. Ensure that directors regularly visit key facilities and meet key customers. They should attend selected company meetings so they can form an independent feel for what's really going on. Provide them an opportunity to offer advice and counsel in context.

6. **Move beyond compliance.** Compliance is a cost of doing business. But if that's your board's focus, you're missing the boat. Get in compliance and then get on with building a better business. Don't let compliance issues dominate the agenda.

7. **Strive for transparency.** Reporting requirements have been expanded considerably by SOX, and most companies view these requirements as an onerous burden. However, transparency engenders trust in management, engages and generates a sense of ownership in employees, and mitigates the type of radical swings in stock price that occur when unexpected news surfaces. The tendency is to hold information close-to-the-vest so it's not used against you by the competition. The market soon learns how to read corporate news releases and values organizations that are forthright and honest in delivering news to the investment community, even news that isn't required by securities law but is meaningful to the individual investor.

8. **Seek balance on the board.** There is always a dynamic tension in corporate governance. Directors who own stock, who have skin in the game, are going to be naturally more motivated to protect the interest of investors. Independence in directors is also valued to protect against the temptation to stretch ethical conduct in the pursuit of wealth. An effective and healthy board balances ownership and independence. No one constituency dominates decisions. Minority and noninstitutional investors are heard. The key is balance. The board has to protect the investors but also must consider the community and other constituents. There must be balance between oversight roles and advising roles. When anything dominates—a particular board profile, a particular shareholder constituency, or a particular board function—corporate governance becomes dysfunctional.

146

9. **Engage the board in talent management.** For multiple reasons, get the board deeply involved in succession and the broader issue of talent management. Although the board generally concentrates on CEO succession, it would be healthy to look broader at the bigger issue of C-suite succession. There can be 20 or more C-level jobs depending upon the organization and industry. The quality of the C-suite is indicative of the overall quality of the business. Research has attributed as much as 40% of the success of an organization to quality of the people working from the C-suite. Have a board member or two attend the annual people reviews. Ensure that directors review the overall talent management system. Ask directors to teach in the learning center. Select a board member or two because of their skills and history at developing leaders.

10. **Seek outside advice and counsel.** Look for answers wherever you can find them. In today's fast-paced and global marketplace, the answers are not always going to be inside the organization. Look to the outside to supplement internal resources. "Open Innovation" is a term promoted by Henry Chesbrough, a professor and executive director at the Center for Open Innovation at Berkeley. The idea behind open innovation is that in a global world of widely distributed knowledge, individual companies cannot afford to rely entirely on their own internal resources. Organizations should, in addition to their own efforts, use external experts wherever they reside. Major advances in electronic technology have facilitated the easy exchange of information. Apply strategic criteria to outside resources. Select resources the same way you would select top management candidates. Apply rigor and discipline. Act on the advice and counsel you pay for. Don't engage outside expertise if you have no intention of heeding their advice. When you engage outside resources, create goals and mission statements for the project. Set time limits and delivery dates. Manage costs like you would for any other business activity. Interview the individual consultants for value and fit. Balance fit with the possibility of contribution. Make sure the outside experts have full access. Help craft the final report to increase the probability of acceptance and execution without hampering the fidelity of the advice. View outside resources as strategic partners. Form trusting and long-term relationships with a small number of outside firms.

SUGGESTED READINGS

Carter, C. B., & Lorsch, J. W. (2003). *Back to the drawing board: Designing corporate boards for a complex world*. Boston, MA: Harvard Business School Press.

Carver, J. (2006). *Boards that make a difference*. San Francisco, CA: Jossey-Bass.

Carver, J., & Oliver, C. (2002). *Corporate boards that create value*. San Francisco, CA: Jossey-Bass.

Charan, R. (1989). *Boards at work: How corporate boards create competitive advantage*. San Francisco, CA: Jossey-Bass.

Charan, R. (2005). *Boards that deliver: Advancing corporate governance from compliance to competitive advantage*. San Francisco, CA: Jossey-Bass.

Chesbrough, Henry William (2003). *Open innovation: The new imperative for creating and profiting from technology*. Boston, MA: Harvard Business School Press.

Colley, J. L., Doyle, J. L., Stettinius, W., & Logan, G. (2003). *Corporate governance*. New York, NY: McGraw-Hill.

Conger, J. A., Lawler, E. E., III, & Finegold, D. (2001). *Corporate boards: New strategies for adding value at the top*. New York, NY: Jossey-Bass.

Eadie, D. (2000). *Extraordinary board leadership: The seven keys to high-impact governance*. Gaithersburg, Maryland: Aspen Publishers, Inc.

Lawler, E., III, Finegold, D., Benson, G., & Conger, J. (2002). Adding value in the boardroom. *Sloan Management Review, 43*(2), 92-93.

Lerer, L. (2006, December 6). The year's biggest hires, fires and retires. *Forbes*. Retrieved January 20, 2007, from http://www.forbes.com/2006/12/06/leadership-managing-careers-lead-careers-cx_ll_1206hfr06.html

Nadler, D. A., (2005). *Building better boards: A blueprint for effective governance*. San Francisco, CA: Jossey-Bass.

Ramos, M. (2006). *How to comply with Sarbanes-Oxley Section 404: Assessing the effectiveness of internal control*. Hoboken, NJ: John Wiley & Sons, Inc.

Roberts, J., McNulty, T., & Stiles, P. (2006). Beyond agency conceptions of the work of the non-executive director: Creating accountability in the boardroom. *British Journal of Management, 16*, 5-26.

Salmon, W. J., Lorsch, J. W., Donaldson, G., Pound, J., Conger, J. A., Finegold, D., & Lawler, E. E. (2000). *Harvard business review on corporate governance*. Boston, MA: Harvard Business School Press.

Shultz, S. (2005). *Board book: Making your corporate board a strategic force in your company's success.* New York, NY: AMACOM.

Stack, J., & Burlingham, B. (2003). *A stake in the outcome: Building a culture of ownership for the long-term success of your business.* New York, NY: Random House.

Tarantino, A. (2006). *Manager's guide to compliance: Sarbanes-Oxley, COSO, ERM, COBIT, IFRS, BASEL II, OMB's A-123, ASX 10, OECD principles, Turnbull guidance, best practices, and case studies.* Hoboken, NJ: John Wiley & Sons, Inc.

Ward, R. D. (2000). *Improving corporate boards: The boardroom insider guidebook.* New York, NY: John Wiley & Sons, Inc.

DIMENSION VIII: GOVERNANCE

T: MANAGE THE BEST WAY

95 STRATEGIC EFFECTIVENESS ARCHITECT™ ITEMS
BY DIMENSION AND CLUSTER

Dimension I: Strategic Accuracy and Clarity
Cluster A: Focusing on Core Organizational and Leadership Capabilities
1. Clearly understand the business(es) we are in and want to be in.
21. Know what our core technical/functional capabilities and unique strengths are.
41. Understand what our core leadership capabilities and unique strengths are.
61. Understand what our core organizational capabilities and unique strengths are.
79. Have a business strategy built around and aligned with our core organizational capabilities.
90. Build or acquire the core business or organizational capabilities that are required, given our strategic outlook, and discard outmoded ones.

Cluster B: Focusing on Customers
2. Know who our most profitable customers are.
22. Customize and tailor our products and services to fit key customers.
42. Understand our customers and their needs.
62. Maintain strong key customer connectedness and relationships.
80. Have a process for gathering and acting on customer feedback and suggestions.

Cluster C: Having a Competitive Strategy
3. Have a clear point of view about the future of our industry and how we position ourselves in it to win.
23. Assess competitor strategies and capabilities.
43. Have a viable and successful annual business planning process.
63. Make competitive product and marketplace decisions.
81. Have a strategy in place to grow sustainable revenue and profitability over the long-term.

Dimension II: Strategy Execution
Cluster D: Aligning with Strategy
4. Continually shape the organization's structure and work flows to meet the changes and challenges of our marketplace.
24. Apply total work systems (e.g., TQM/ISO/Six Sigma) where needed.
44. Efficiently and effectively communicate our strategy to all employees.
64. Align people policies, practices, and programs to support our business strategy.
82. Identify the management and leadership competencies that our strategy requires.

Dimension II: Strategy Execution (continued)

Cluster E: Execution and Decision Making

5. Use our strategy to guide decision making.

25. Make tough decisions quickly.

45. Exhibit unrelenting and aggressive competitiveness in the marketplace.

65. Execute and implement difficult strategies rapidly and effectively.

83. Allocate proportionate resources to our most critical products and services.

Dimension III: Managing Innovation and Change

Cluster F: Innovation Leadership

6. Know what and where to innovate.

26. Innovate decisively and in a timely fashion.

46. Leverage technology productively.

66. Create breakthrough products and services.

Cluster G: Organizational Learning

7. Generate new ways to do things.

27. Freely discard and change policies, practices, and processes to respond to new challenges.

47. Generalize and transfer critical knowledge and ideas seamlessly across boundaries and between units, functions, and geographies inside the organization.

67. Have a well-supported process and culture of challenging the status quo.

84. Generate impactful ideas through experimentation, continuous improvement, or benchmarking.

91. Rapidly and effectively adjust to crises, economic turmoil, natural disasters, acts of terrorism, and other unanticipated disruptions.

Dimension IV: Attracting/Retaining/Motivating Talent

Cluster H: Upgrading the Workforce

8. Continuously upgrade our workforce by bringing in new talent, keeping the best, and releasing the lowest performers.

28. Have a well-supported process in place to orient new employees to our culture.

48. Invest in building existing talent through training, development, and work experiences.

68. Promote the right people.

85. Have a feedback-rich environment in which everyone knows where he or she stands.

Dimension IV: Attracting/Retaining/Motivating Talent (continued)

Cluster I: Engaging Employees

9. Have loyal and committed employees.
29. Have strong trust between our top management and employees.
49. Make employees feel like stakeholders.
69. Measure and respond to employee engagement data.

Cluster J: Accountability and Rewards

10. Translate individual and collective goals and objectives into performance standards.
30. Lay out clear accountabilities and consequences for everyone in the organization.
50. Use compensation as a tool to focus and drive performance.
70. Have a significant amount of pay at risk for top management.
86. Reward people differentially based upon their overall contribution to the organization.
92. Concentrate on measuring results with a balanced measures scorecard.

Dimension V: Leveraging a Productive Culture

Cluster K: Leveraging Culture

11. Use corporate culture as a tool for linking with key customers and strategy.
31. Adapt our culture to the brand or identification of the firm in the mind of the customer.
51. Translate the desired culture into a set of employee behaviors and practices.
71. Model our core values and culture.

Cluster L: Managing Communication

12. Create a shared mind-set at all levels and in all employees to focus their efforts.
32. Keep communications focused on the right messages.
52. Use multiple and innovative methods to share information.
72. Have an effective communication process in place for keeping our employees informed on important issues.

Cluster M: Collaborating Across Boundaries

13. Work well in teams when required.
33. Support teams where critical and appropriate.
53. Use cross-functional/unit work teams and task forces to address problems.
73. Seamlessly coordinate work across boundaries (departments, functions, geographies, and business).
87. Move decision-making authority as close to the action as possible.
93. Effectively work through internal conflicts with minimum damage.

Dimension V: Leveraging a Productive Culture (continued)

Cluster N: Managing Diversity

14. Have the diversity in our workforce and among top decision makers that aligns with the labor market and our customers.

34. Make effective use of diversity (of thought, opinion, gender, ethnicity, etc.) in our workforce.

54. Anticipate and effectively adjust for demographic changes and diversity in our workforce.

Dimension VI: Managing Profitability and Delivering Value

Cluster O: Basis for Competitive Advantage

15. Be the price/value leader in our marketplace.

35. Be the low-cost producer or provider in our marketplace.

55. Be the premium/quality niche provider.

74. Be the customer-service leader in our marketplace.

88. Continuously enter, create, and grow new markets.

Cluster P: Supply Chain Management (from Raw Material to Customer)

16. Use our edge in supply chain management to compete.

36. Have a set of metrics to monitor our supply chain efficiently and effectively.

56. Have more effective supplier and vendor relationships than our competitors.

75. Seek out and make joint ventures and strategic partnerships work.

Cluster Q: Running a Profitable Business

17. Improve profitability and business results every year.

37. Have high productivity; use resources efficiently.

57. Have predictable financial results.

Cluster R: Creating and Sustaining Value

18. Deliver value to our investors and other relevant shareholders.

38. Deliver value to our customers.

58. Deliver value (workplace, job, career) to our employees.

76. Deliver value to the communities in which we operate.

Dimension VII: Developing Future Leaders

Cluster S: Filling the Talent Bench

19. Have a well-supported process in place to identify and develop the next generation of leaders.

39. Move people across functional, geographic, and business unit boundaries for development as future leaders.

59. Accurately differentiate our people based on potential (high, moderate, low).

77. Accurately distinguish between our top, middle, and bottom performers.

89. Have senior management and/or the board actively engaged in our talent management process.

94. Use job assignments to build new skills in high-potential employees.

95. Acquire talent from outside as needed for key positions.

Dimension VIII: Governance

Cluster T: Managing in the Best Way

20. Select and shape a board of directors that adds value.

40. Actively engage the board of directors in the business.

60. Effectively utilize outside resources (auditors, consultants, advisors, experts).

78. Manage the enterprise with appropriate transparency and openness.

MAPPING TO: THE LEADERSHIP ARCHITECT®
COMPETENCY LIBRARY

Each of the 95 STRATEGIC EFFECTIVENESS ARCHITECT™ items, the 20 clusters, and the 8 dimensions are mapped back into the LEADERSHIP ARCHITECT® Competency Library. This library further defines individual behaviors which leaders and managers need in order to be skilled in that organizational behavior.

The lists below show the mapping between the 20 clusters (A–T) contained in the STRATEGIC EFFECTIVENESS ARCHITECT™ toolkit and the 67 competencies contained in the LEADERSHIP ARCHITECT® Competency Library. For each competency, the strength of the connection to the cluster is indicated—Strong, Some, and Light. For example, in Cluster A below, #2. Dealing with Ambiguity is one of the most strongly mapped (most connected) competencies related to Cluster A, and #52. Process Management is related to a lesser extent.

Dimension I: Strategic Accuracy and Clarity
Cluster A: Focusing on Core Organizational and Leadership Capabilities
Item 1. Clearly understand the business(es) we are in and want to be in.

Strong	Some	Light
2. Dealing with Ambiguity	15. Customer Focus	28. Innovation Management
5. Business Acumen	17. Decision Quality	30. Intellectual Horsepower
46. Perspective	50. Priority Setting	38. Organizational Agility
51. Problem Solving	63. Total Work Systems	52. Process Management
58. Strategic Agility		

Item 21. Know what our core technical/functional capabilities and unique strengths are.

Strong	Some	Light
5. Business Acumen	2. Dealing with Ambiguity	15. Customer Focus
51. Problem Solving	24. Functional/Technical Skills	17. Decision Quality
52. Process Management	32. Learning on the Fly	33. Listening
56. Sizing Up People	46. Perspective	38. Organizational Agility
58. Strategic Agility	59. Managing Through Systems	50. Priority Setting
		61. Technical Learning

Item 41. Understand what our core leadership capabilities and unique strengths are.

Strong	Some	Light
5. Business Acumen	2. Dealing with Ambiguity	15. Customer Focus
46. Perspective	17. Decision Quality	32. Learning on the Fly
56. Sizing Up People	50. Priority Setting	33. Listening
58. Strategic Agility	51. Problem Solving	38. Organizational Agility
64. Understanding Others	65. Managing Vision and Purpose	

Item 61. Understand what our core organizational capabilities and unique strengths are.

Strong	Some	Light
5. Business Acumen	15. Customer Focus	2. Dealing with Ambiguity
24. Functional/Technical Skills	17. Decision Quality	32. Learning on the Fly
38. Organizational Agility	51. Problem Solving	33. Listening
46. Perspective	58. Strategic Agility	63. Total Work Systems
52. Process Management		

Cluster A: Focusing on Core Organizational and Leadership Capabilities (continued)

Item 79. Have a business strategy built around and aligned with our core organizational capabilities.

Strong	Some	Light
5. Business Acumen	2. Dealing with Ambiguity	12. Conflict Management
46. Perspective	17. Decision Quality	34. Managerial Courage
47. Planning	50. Priority Setting	38. Organizational Agility
56. Sizing Up People	52. Process Management	51. Problem Solving
58. Strategic Agility	65. Managing Vision and Purpose	

Item 90. Build or acquire the core business or organizational capabilities that are required, given our strategic outlook, and discard outmoded ones.

Strong	Some	Light
17. Decision Quality	2. Dealing with Ambiguity	12. Conflict Management
46. Perspective	5. Business Acumen	14. Creativity
47. Planning	9. Command Skills	15. Customer Focus
50. Priority Setting	19. Developing Direct Reports and Others	43. Perseverance
56. Sizing Up People	28. Innovation Management	51. Problem Solving
58. Strategic Agility	34. Managerial Courage	52. Process Management
65. Managing Vision and Purpose	60. Building Effective Teams	61. Technical Learning

Cluster B: Focusing on Customers

Item 2. Know who our most profitable customers are.

Strong	Some	Light
5. Business Acumen	46. Perspective	17. Decision Quality
15. Customer Focus	51. Problem Solving	32. Learning on the Fly
53. Drive for Results	58. Strategic Agility	33. Listening
		64. Understanding Others

Item 22. Customize and tailor our products and services to fit key customers.

Strong	Some	Light
15. Customer Focus	5. Business Acumen	14. Creativity
17. Decision Quality	24. Functional/Technical Skills	32. Learning on the Fly
28. Innovation Management	47. Planning	38. Organizational Agility
33. Listening	51. Problem Solving	46. Perspective
37. Negotiating	63. Total Work Systems	58. Strategic Agility
52. Process Management	65. Managing Vision and Purpose	64. Understanding Others

Item 42. Understand our customers and their needs.

Strong	Some	Light
15. Customer Focus	5. Business Acumen	2. Dealing with Ambiguity
32. Learning on the Fly	31. Interpersonal Savvy	3. Approachability
33. Listening	51. ProblemSolving	24. Functional/TechnicalSkills
46. Perspective	58. Strategic Agility	38. Organizational Agility
56. Sizing Up People	64. Understanding Others	61. Technical Learning

Cluster B: Focusing on Customers (continued)

Item 62. Maintain strong key customer connectedness and relationships.

Strong	Some	Light
12. Conflict Management	2. Dealing with Ambiguity	21. Managing Diversity
15. Customer Focus	16. Timely Decision Making	35. Managing and
31. Interpersonal Savvy	27. Informing	Measuring Work
33. Listening	29. Integrity and Trust	37. Negotiating
36. Motivating Others	38. Organizational Agility	47. Planning
41. Patience	39. Organizing	48. Political Savvy
51. Problem Solving	52. Process Management	62. Time Management
56. Sizing Up People	53. Drive for Results	64. Understanding Others

Item 80. Have a process for gathering and acting on customer feedback and suggestions.

Strong	Some	Light
12. Conflict Management	1. Action Oriented	11. Composure
15. Customer Focus	17. Decision Quality	32. Learning on the Fly
16. Timely Decision Making	36. Motivating Others	37. Negotiating
33. Listening	41. Patience	38. Organizational Agility
52. Process Management	50. Priority Setting	47. Planning
56. Sizing Up People	51. Problem Solving	53. Drive for Results
64. Understanding Others	59. Managing Through Systems	61. Technical Learning

Cluster C: Having a Competitive Strategy

Item 3. Have a clear point of view about the future of our industry and how we position ourselves in it to win.

Strong	Some	Light
2. Dealing with Ambiguity	17. Decision Quality	21. Managing Diversity
5. Business Acumen	50. Priority Setting	30. Intellectual Horsepower
15. Customer Focus	51. Problem Solving	48. Political Savvy
46. Perspective	64. Understanding Others	57. Standing Alone
58. Strategic Agility		65. Managing Vision and Purpose

Item 23. Assess competitor strategies and capabilities.

Strong	Some	Light
5. Business Acumen	2. Dealing with Ambiguity	15. Customer Focus
32. Learning on the Fly	17. Decision Quality	24. Functional/Technical Skills
38. Organizational Agility	51. Problem Solving	30. Intellectual Horsepower
46. Perspective	52. Process Management	61. Technical Learning
56. Sizing Up People	58. Strategic Agility	64. Understanding Others

Item 43. Have a viable and successful annual business planning process.

Strong	Some	Light
5. Business Acumen	24. Functional/Technical Skills	2. Dealing with Ambiguity
15. Customer Focus	34. Managerial Courage	17. Decision Quality
47. Planning	35. Managing and Measuring Work	37. Negotiating
50. Priority Setting	52. Process Management	46. Perspective
51. Problem Solving	53. Drive for Results	58. Strategic Agility

Cluster C: Having a Competitive Strategy (continued)

Item 63. Make competitive product and marketplace decisions.

Strong	Some	Light
5. Business Acumen	2. Dealing with Ambiguity	14. Creativity
15. Customer Focus	9. Command Skills	16. Timely Decision Making
28. Innovation Management	17. Decision Quality	24. Functional/Technical Skills
33. Listening	32. Learning on the Fly	47. Planning
46. Perspective	34. Managerial Courage	61. Technical Learning
51. Problem Solving	50. Priority Setting	64. Understanding Others
	58. Strategic Agility	

Item 81. Have a strategy in place to grow sustainable revenue and profitability over the long-term.

Strong	Some	Light
5. Business Acumen	2. Dealing with Ambiguity	14. Creativity
28. Innovation Management	15. Customer Focus	21. Managing Diversity
46. Perspective	30. Intellectual Horsepower	64. Understanding Others
50. Priority Setting	52. Process Management	
51. Problem Solving		
58. Strategic Agility		

Dimension II: Strategy Execution
Cluster D: Aligning with Strategy

Item 4. Continually shape the organization's structure and work flows to meet the changes and challenges of our marketplace.

Strong	Some	Light
2. Dealing with Ambiguity	15. Customer Focus	1. Action Oriented
12. Conflict Management	16. Timely Decision Making	5. Business Acumen
47. Planning	28. Innovation Management	35. Managing and
50. Priority Setting	32. Learning on the Fly	Measuring Work
51. Problem Solving	38. Organizational Agility	46. Perspective
52. Process Management	39. Organizing	59. Managing Through Systems
63. Total Work Systems		61. Technical Learning

Item 24. Apply total work systems (e.g., TQM/ISO/Six Sigma) where needed.

Strong	Some	Light
47. Planning	17. Decision Quality	5. Business Acumen
51. Problem Solving	41. Patience	35. Managing and
52. Process Management	50. Priority Setting	Measuring Work
63. Total Work Systems	59. Managing	43. Perseverance
	Through Systems	61. Technical Learning

Cluster D: Aligning with Strategy (continued)

Item 44. Efficiently and effectively communicate our strategy to all employees.

Strong	Some	Light
27. Informing	2. Dealing with Ambiguity	12. Conflict Management
32. Learning on the Fly	5. Business Acumen	26. Humor
36. Motivating Others	33. Listening	29. Integrity and Trust
49. Presentation Skills	41. Patience	52. Process Management
56. Sizing Up People	46. Perspective	60. Building Effective Teams
65. Managing Vision	58. Strategic Agility	64. Understanding Others
and Purpose	67. Written Communications	

Item 64. Align people policies, practices, and programs to support our business strategy.

Strong	Some	Light
35. Managing and	5. Business Acumen	17. Decision Quality
Measuring Work	38. Organizational Agility	39. Organizing
51. Problem Solving	47. Planning	46. Perspective
52. Process Management	50. Priority Setting	63. Total Work Systems
58. Strategic Agility	59. Managing	
65. Managing Vision	Through Systems	
and Purpose		

Item 82. Identify the management and leadership competencies that our strategy requires.

Strong	Some	Light
2. Dealing with Ambiguity	17. Decision Quality	5. Business Acumen
46. Perspective	25. Hiring and Staffing	52. Process Management
51. Problem Solving	50. Priority Setting	55. Self-Knowledge
58. Strategic Agility	56. Sizing Up People	64. Understanding Others

Cluster E: Execution and Decision Making

Item 5. Use our strategy to guide decision making.

Strong	Some	Light
5. Business Acumen	17. Decision Quality	2. Dealing with Ambiguity
47. Planning	35. Managing and	30. Intellectual Horsepower
50. Priority Setting	Measuring Work	40. Dealing with Paradox
53. Drive for Results	46. Perspective	65. Managing Vision and Purpose
58. Strategic Agility	51. Problem Solving	
	52. Process Management	

Item 25. Make tough decisions quickly.

Strong	Some	Light
1. Action Oriented	34. Managerial Courage	9. Command Skills
2. Dealing with Ambiguity	36. Motivating Others	17. Decision Quality
12. Conflict Management	40. Dealing with Paradox	43. Perseverance
16. Timely Decision Making	51. Problem Solving	46. Perspective
32. Learning on the Fly	53. Drive for Results	58. Strategic Agility
50. Priority Setting	57. Standing Alone	62. Time Management

Cluster E: Execution and Decision Making (continued)

Item 45. Exhibit unrelenting and aggressive competitiveness in the marketplace.

Strong	Some	Light
1. Action Oriented	12. Conflict Management	2. Dealing with Ambiguity
9. Command Skills	15. Customer Focus	5. Business Acumen
16. Timely Decision Making	34. Managerial Courage	39. Organizing
32. Learning on the Fly	37. Negotiating	57. Standing Alone
53. Drive for Results	43. Perseverance	

Item 65. Execute and implement difficult strategies rapidly and effectively.

Strong	Some	Light
12. Conflict Management	1. Action Oriented	13. Confronting Direct Reports
36. Motivating Others	9. Command Skills	38. Organizational Agility
50. Priority Setting	16. Timely Decision Making	46. Perspective
51. Problem Solving	27. Informing	47. Planning
52. Process Management	32. Learning on the Fly	58. Strategic Agility
53. Drive for Results	34. Managerial Courage	60. Building Effective Teams
56. Sizing Up People	39. Organizing	
65. Managing Vision and Purpose		

Item 83. Allocate proportionate resources to our most critical products and services.

Strong	Some	Light
12. Conflict Management	17. Decision Quality	2. Dealing with Ambiguity
37. Negotiating	38. Organizational Agility	35. Managing and Measuring Work
47. Planning	39. Organizing	40. Dealing with Paradox
50. Priority Setting	52. Process Management	46. Perspective
51. Problem Solving	58. Strategic Agility	65. Managing Vision and Purpose

Dimension III: Managing Innovation and Change
Cluster F: Innovation Leadership

Item 6. Know what and where to innovate.

Strong	Some	Light
2. Dealing with Ambiguity	5. Business Acumen	14. Creativity
15. Customer Focus	17. Decision Quality	30. Intellectual Horsepower
28. Innovation Management	32. Learning on the Fly	40. Dealing with Paradox
33. Listening	51. Problem Solving	64. Understanding Others
46. Perspective	58. Strategic Agility	65. Managing Vision and Purpose
50. Priority Setting		

Item 26. Innovate decisively and in a timely fashion.

Strong	Some	Light
1. Action Oriented	2. Dealing with Ambiguity	14. Creativity
9. Command Skills	28. Innovation Management	32. Learning on the Fly
12. Conflict Management	34. Managerial Courage	36. Motivating Others
16. Timely Decision Making	39. Organizing	37. Negotiating
51. Problem Solving	50. Priority Setting	53. Drive for Results
57. Standing Alone	52. Process Management	61. Technical Learning

Cluster F: Innovation Leadership (continued)

Item 46. Leverage technology productively.

Strong	Some	Light
28. Innovation Management	2. Dealing with Ambiguity	15. Customer Focus
46. Perspective	5. Business Acumen	24. Functional/Technical Skills
51. Problem Solving	17. Decision Quality	39. Organizing
52. Process Management	32. Learning on the Fly	47. Planning
53. Drive for Results	50. Priority Setting	65. Managing Vision and Purpose
61. Technical Learning	58. Strategic Agility	

Item 66. Create breakthrough products and services.

Strong	Some	Light
14. Creativity	1. Action Oriented	5. Business Acumen
28. Innovation Management	2. Dealing with Ambiguity	15. Customer Focus
33. Listening	16. Timely Decision Making	34. Managerial Courage
46. Perspective	32. Learning on the Fly	43. Perseverance
51. Problem Solving	36. Motivating Others	57. Standing Alone
52. Process Management	50. Priority Setting	58. Strategic Agility
61. Technical Learning		

Cluster G: Organizational Learning

Item 7. Generate new ways to do things.

Strong	Some	Light
2. Dealing with Ambiguity	1. Action Oriented	9. Command Skills
14. Creativity	12. Conflict Management	28. Innovation Management
51. Problem Solving	33. Listening	32. Learning on the Fly
52. Process Management	43. Perseverance	34. Managerial Courage
57. Standing Alone	61. Technical Learning	36. Motivating Others

Item 27. Freely discard and change policies, practices, and processes to respond to new challenges.

Strong	Some	Light
2. Dealing with Ambiguity	1. Action Oriented	32. Learning on the Fly
9. Command Skills	8. Comfort Around	36. Motivating Others
12. Conflict Management	Higher Management	46. Perspective
16. Timely Decision Making	51. Problem Solving	50. Priority Setting
34. Managerial Courage	52. Process Management	63. Total Work Systems
40. Dealing with Paradox	57. Standing Alone	
53. Drive for Results		

Item 47. Generalize and transfer critical knowledge and ideas seamlessly across boundaries and between units, functions, and geographies inside the organization.

Strong	Some	Light
12. Conflict Management	31. Interpersonal Savvy	2. Dealing with Ambiguity
27. Informing	36. Motivating Others	18. Delegation
32. Learning on the Fly	37. Negotiating	21. Managing Diversity
33. Listening	38. Organizational Agility	29. Integrity and Trust
41. Patience	40. Dealing with Paradox	45. Personal Learning
42. Peer Relationships	52. Process Management	60. Building Effective Teams
48. Political Savvy	56. Sizing Up People	64. Understanding Others
	61. Technical Learning	

Cluster G: Organizational Learning (continued)

Item 67. Have a well-supported process and culture of challenging the status quo.

Strong	Some	Light
2. Dealing with Ambiguity	4. Boss Relationships	11. Composure
8. Comfort Around Higher Management	37. Negotiating	27. Informing
9. Command Skills	43. Perseverance	29. Integrity and Trust
12. Conflict Management	51. Problem Solving	42. Peer Relationships
33. Listening	53. Drive for Results	48. Political Savvy
34. Managerial Courage		
57. Standing Alone		

Item 84. Generate impactful ideas through experimentation, continuous improvement, or benchmarking.

Strong	Some	Light
14. Creativity	2. Dealing with Ambiguity	1. Action Oriented
32. Learning on the Fly	12. Conflict Management	5. Business Acumen
33. Listening	28. Innovation Management	36. Motivating Others
46. Perspective	52. Process Management	43. Perseverance
51. Problem Solving	61. Technical Learning	53. Drive for Results
		63. Total Work Systems

Item 91. Rapidly and effectively adjust to crises, economic turmoil, natural disasters, acts of terrorism, and other unanticipated disruptions.

Strong	Some	Light
1. Action Oriented	12. Conflict Management	11. Composure
2. Dealing with Ambiguity	36. Motivating Others	37. Negotiating
9. Command Skills	39. Organizing	43. Perseverance
16. Timely Decision Making	46. Perspective	48. Political Savvy
27. Informing		
32. Learning on the Fly		
40. Dealing with Paradox		
50. Priority Setting		
51. Problem Solving		

Dimension IV: Attracting/Retaining/Motivating Talent
Cluster H: Upgrading the Workforce

Item 8. Continuously upgrade our workforce by bringing in new talent, keeping the best, and releasing the lowest performers.

Strong	Some	Light
13. Confronting Direct Reports	2. Dealing with Ambiguity	22. Ethics and Values
16. Timely Decision Making	9. Command Skills	23. Fairness to Direct Reports
25. Hiring and Staffing	12. Conflict Management	46. Perspective
34. Managerial Courage	17. Decision Quality	57. Standing Alone
36. Motivating Others	35. Managing and Measuring Work	58. Strategic Agility
56. Sizing Up People	40. Dealing with Paradox	

Cluster H: Upgrading the Workforce (continued)

Item 28. Have a well-supported process in place to orient new employees to our culture.

Strong	Some	Light
27. Informing	19. Developing Direct	3. Approachability
33. Listening	Reports and Others	7. Caring About Direct Reports
36. Motivating Others	29. Integrity and Trust	21. Managing Diversity
47. Planning	52. Process Management	41. Patience
56. Sizing Up People	60. Building Effective Teams	49. Presentation Skills
65. Managing Vision	64. Understanding Others	62. Time Management
and Purpose		

Item 48. Invest in building existing talent through training, development, and work experiences.

Strong	Some	Light
18. Delegation	27. Informing	12. Conflict Management
19. Developing Direct	36. Motivating Others	13. Confronting Direct Reports
Reports and Others	41. Patience	17. Decision Quality
20. Directing Others	50. Priority Setting	33. Listening
47. Planning	62. Time Management	40. Dealing with Paradox
56. Sizing Up People		
58. Strategic Agility		

Item 68. Promote the right people.

Strong	Some	Light
2. Dealing with Ambiguity	9. Command Skills	21. Managing Diversity
13. Confronting	12. Conflict Management	23. Fairness to Direct Reports
Direct Reports	33. Listening	35. Managing and
17. Decision Quality	46. Perspective	Measuring Work
25. Hiring and Staffing	53. Drive for Results	37. Negotiating
56. Sizing Up People	65. Managing Vision	57. Standing Alone
58. Strategic Agility	and Purpose	

Item 85. Have a feedback-rich environment in which everyone knows where he or she stands.

Strong	Some	Light
12. Conflict Management	16. Timely Decision Making	2. Dealing with Ambiguity
13. Confronting	19. Developing Direct	9. Command Skills
Direct Reports	Reports and Others	11. Composure
20. Directing Others	29. Integrity and Trust	23. Fairness to Direct Reports
27. Informing	31. Interpersonal Savvy	41. Patience
34. Managerial Courage	33. Listening	64. Understanding Others
35. Managing and	56. Sizing Up People	
Measuring Work	57. Standing Alone	
62. Time Management		

Cluster I: Engaging Employees

Item 9. Have loyal and committed employees.

Strong	Some	Light
18. Delegation	12. Conflict Management	3. Approachability
19. Developing Direct Reports and Others	20. Directing Others	7. Caring About Direct Reports
23. Fairness to Direct Reports	22. Ethics and Values	9. Command Skills
27. Informing	29. Integrity and Trust	10. Compassion
33. Listening	36. Motivating Others	21. Managing Diversity
60. Building Effective Teams	41. Patience	31. Interpersonal Savvy
65. Managing Vision and Purpose	64. Understanding Others	53. Drive for Results

Item 29. Have strong trust between our top management and employees.

Strong	Some	Light
12. Conflict Management	17. Decision Quality	3. Approachability
18. Delegation	22. Ethics and Values	7. Caring About Direct Reports
27. Informing	34. Managerial Courage	9. Command Skills
29. Integrity and Trust	36. Motivating Others	19. Developing Direct Reports and Others
33. Listening	41. Patience	20. Directing Others
65. Managing Vision and Purpose	44. Personal Disclosure	23. Fairness to Direct Reports
	60. Building Effective Teams	57. Standing Alone

Item 49. Make employees feel like stakeholders.

Strong	Some	Light
18. Delegation	7. Caring About Direct Reports	3. Approachability
27. Informing	10. Compassion	21. Managing Diversity
33. Listening	19. Developing Direct Reports and Others	22. Ethics and Values
36. Motivating Others	65. Managing Vision and Purpose	29. Integrity and Trust
60. Building Effective Teams		23. Fairness to Direct Reports
		64. Understanding Others

Item 69. Measure and respond to employee engagement data.

Strong	Some	Light
1. Action Oriented	7. Caring About Direct Reports	21. Managing Diversity
12. Conflict Management	27. Informing	36. Motivating Others
16. Timely Decision Making	35. Managing and Measuring Work	38. Organizational Agility
33. Listening	39. Organizing	47. Planning
41. Patience	51. Problem Solving	50. Priority Setting
64. Understanding Others	62. Time Management	56. Sizing Up People

Cluster J: Accountability and Rewards

Item 10. Translate individual and collective goals and objectives into performance standards.

Strong	Some	Light
20. Directing Others	5. Business Acumen	13. Confronting Direct Reports
35. Managing and Measuring Work	27. Informing	37. Negotiating
47. Planning	53. Drive for Results	52. Process Management
50. Priority Setting	65. Managing Vision and Purpose	56. Sizing Up People
51. Problem Solving		

Item 30. Lay out clear accountabilities and consequences for everyone in the organization.

Strong	Some	Light
20. Directing Others	39. Organizing	12. Conflict Management
27. Informing	50. Priority Setting	13. Confronting Direct Reports
35. Managing and Measuring Work	52. Process Management	18. Delegation
47. Planning	53. Drive for Results	56. Sizing Up People
	65. Managing Vision and Purpose	62. Time Management

Item 50. Use compensation as a tool to focus and drive performance.

Strong	Some	Light
2. Dealing with Ambiguity	17. Decision Quality	20. Directing Others
12. Conflict Management	27. Informing	23. Fairness to Direct Reports
13. Confronting Direct Reports	36. Motivating Others	37. Negotiating
35. Managing and Measuring Work	50. Priority Setting	47. Planning
56. Sizing Up People	51. Problem Solving	52. Process Management

Item 70. Have a significant amount of pay at risk for top management.

Strong	Some	Light
35. Managing and Measuring Work	2. Dealing with Ambiguity	5. Business Acumen
53. Drive for Results	12. Conflict Management	37. Negotiating
56. Sizing Up People	13. Confronting Direct Reports	50. Priority Setting
58. Strategic Agility	65. Managing Vision and Purpose	

Item 86. Reward people differentially based upon their overall contribution to the organization.

Strong	Some	Light
13. Confronting Direct Reports	5. Business Acumen	2. Dealing with Ambiguity
20. Directing Others	12. Conflict Management	23. Fairness to Direct Reports
35. Managing and Measuring Work	36. Motivating Others	34. Managerial Courage
53. Drive for Results	37. Negotiating	65. Managing Vision and Purpose
56. Sizing Up People		

Cluster J: Accountability and Rewards (continued)

Item 92. Concentrate on measuring results with a balanced measures scorecard.

Strong	Some	Light
5. Business Acumen	13. Confronting Direct Reports	2. Dealing with Ambiguity
35. Managing and Measuring Work	34. Managerial Courage	27. Informing
50. Priority Setting	46. Perspective	51. Problem Solving
53. Drive for Results	47. Planning	52. Process Management
56. Sizing Up People		

Dimension V: Leveraging a Productive Culture

Cluster K: Leveraging Culture

Item 11. Use corporate culture as a tool for linking with key customers and strategy.

Strong	Some	Light
15. Customer Focus	2. Dealing with Ambiguity	12. Conflict Management
38. Organizational Agility	46. Perspective	17. Decision Quality
51. Problem Solving	47. Planning	34. Managerial Courage
64. Understanding Others	52. Process Management	40. Dealing with Paradox
65. Managing Vision and Purpose	58. Strategic Agility	60. Building Effective Teams

Item 31. Adapt our culture to the brand or identification of the firm in the mind of the customer.

Strong	Some	Light
15. Customer Focus	2. Dealing with Ambiguity	5. Business Acumen
27. Informing	38. Organizational Agility	48. Political Savvy
33. Listening	46. Perspective	58. Strategic Agility
36. Motivating Others	51. Problem Solving	
64. Understanding Others	52. Process Management	
65. Managing Vision and Purpose	60. Building Effective Teams	

Item 51. Translate the desired culture into a set of employee behaviors and practices.

Strong	Some	Light
35. Managing and Measuring Work	2. Dealing with Ambiguity	22. Ethics and Values
	9. Command Skills	30. Intellectual Horsepower
47. Planning	20. Directing Others	38. Organizational Agility
51. Problem Solving	27. Informing	59. Managing Through Systems
52. Process Management	46. Perspective	62. Time Management
65. Managing Vision and Purpose	50. Priority Setting	

Item 71. Model our core values and culture.

Strong	Some	Light
22. Ethics and Values	29. Integrity and Trust	27. Informing
45. Personal Learning	36. Motivating Others	44. Personal Disclosure
57. Standing Alone	40. Dealing with Paradox	
65. Managing Vision and Purpose		

Cluster L: Managing Communication

Item12. Create a shared mind-set at all levels and in all employees to focus their efforts.

Strong	Some	Light
27. Informing	5. Business Acumen	20. Directing Others
36. Motivating Others	12. Conflict Management	39. Organizing
46. Perspective	22. Ethics and Values	41. Patience
49. Presentation Skills	29. Integrity and Trust	52. Process Management
60. Building Effective Teams	38. Organizational Agility	59. Managing Through Systems
65. Managing Vision	58. Strategic Agility	62. Time Management
and Purpose	64. Understanding Others	67. Written Communications

Item 32. Keep communications focused on the right messages.

Strong	Some	Light
27. Informing	5. Business Acumen	43. Perseverance
47. Planning	46. Perspective	64. Understanding Others
50. Priority Setting	52. Process Management	
65. Managing Vision	58. Strategic Agility	
and Purpose		

Item 52. Use multiple and innovative methods to share information.

Strong	Some	Light
14. Creativity	27. Informing	21. Managing Diversity
36. Motivating Others	28. Innovation Management	38. Organizational Agility
51. ProblemSolving	33. Listening	48. Political Savvy
61. Technical Learning	47. Planning	49. Presentation Skills
64. Understanding Others	52. Process Management	67. Written Communications

Item 72. Have an effective communication process in place for keeping our employees informed on important issues.

Strong	Some	Light
27. Informing	20. Directing Others	38. Organizational Agility
47. Planning	33. Listening	39. Organizing
52. Process Management	36. Motivating Others	49. Presentation Skills
64. Understanding Others	46. Perspective	60. Building Effective Teams
65. Managing Vision	51. Problem Solving	67. Written Communications
and Purpose		

Cluster M: Collaborating Across Boundaries

Item13. Work well in teams when required.

Strong	Some	Light
12. Conflict Management	3. Approachability	2. Dealing with Ambiguity
18. Delegation	27. Informing	21. Managing Diversity
29. Integrity and Trust	31. Interpersonal Savvy	26. Humor
42. Peer Relationships	33. Listening	36. Motivating Others
56. Sizing Up People	41. Patience	37. Negotiating
60. Building Effective Teams	45. Personal Learning	

Cluster M: Collaborating Across Boundaries (continued)

Item 33. Support teams where critical and appropriate.

Strong	Some	Light
18. Delegation	20. Directing Others	2. Dealing with Ambiguity
27. Informing	35. Managing and	12. Conflict Management
33. Listening	Measuring Work	56. Sizing Up People
39. Organizing	36. Motivating Others	64. Understanding Others
60. Building Effective Teams	38. Organizational Agility	
	41. Patience	

Item 53. Use cross-functional/unit work teams and task forces to address problems.

Strong	Some	Light
12. Conflict Management	36. Motivating Others	38. Organizational Agility
18. Delegation	37. Negotiating	48. Political Savvy
27. Informing	39. Organizing	52. Process Management
33. Listening	41. Patience	53. Drive for Results
42. Peer Relationships	51. Problem Solving	56. Sizing Up People
60. Building Effective Teams	59. Managing Through	
	Systems	

Item 73. Seamlessly coordinate work across boundaries (departments, functions, geographies, and business).

Strong	Some	Light
33. Listening	12. Conflict Management	2. Dealing with Ambiguity
38. Organizational Agility	27. Informing	15. Customer Focus
39. Organizing	31. Interpersonal Savvy	18. Delegation
42. Peer Relationships	37. Negotiating	29. Integrity and Trust
48. Political Savvy	47. Planning	36. Motivating Others
52. Process Management	64. Understanding Others	41. Patience
59. Managing Through	65. Managing Vision	50. Priority Setting
Systems	and Purpose	53. Drive for Results

Item 87. Move decision-making authority as close to the action as possible.

Strong	Some	Light
18. Delegation	2. Dealing with Ambiguity	33. Listening
20. Directing Others	15. Customer Focus	36. Motivating Others
27. Informing	50. Priority Setting	39. Organizing
35. Managing and	52. Process Management	41. Patience
Measuring Work	59. Managing Through	51. Problem Solving
56. Sizing Up People	Systems	

Item 93. Effectively work through internal conflicts with minimum damage.

Strong	Some	Light
11. Composure	2. Dealing with Ambiguity	9. Command Skills
12. Conflict Management	29. Integrity and Trust	13. Confronting Direct Reports
31. Interpersonal Savvy	33. Listening	22. Ethics and Values
34. Managerial Courage	36. Motivating Others	38. Organizational Agility
40. Dealing with Paradox	37. Negotiating	41. Patience
51. Problem Solving	45. Personal Learning	42. Peer Relationships
57. Standing Alone	48. Political Savvy	64. Understanding Others

Cluster N: Managing Diversity

Item 14. Have the diversity in our workforce and among top decision makers that aligns with the labor market and our customers.

Strong	Some	Light
21. Managing Diversity	2. Dealing with Ambiguity	33. Listening
25. Hiring and Staffing	19. Developing Direct	48. Political Savvy
46. Perspective	Reports and Others	64. Understanding Others
56. Sizing Up People	23. Fairness to Direct Reports	
58. Strategic Agility	45. Personal Learning	
	57. Standing Alone	

Item 34. Make effective use of diversity (of thought, opinion, gender, ethnicity, etc.) in our workforce.

Strong	Some	Light
3. Approachability	2. Dealing with Ambiguity	18. Delegation
21. Managing Diversity	12. Conflict Management	23. Fairness to Direct Reports
25. Hiring and Staffing	32. Learning on the Fly	40. Dealing with Paradox
33. Listening	36. Motivating Others	44. Personal Disclosure
41. Patience	56. Sizing Up People	45. Personal Learning
46. Perspective	64. Understanding Others	58. Strategic Agility

Item 54. Anticipate and effectively adjust for demographic changes and diversity in our workforce.

Strong	Some	Light
21. Managing Diversity	2. Dealing with Ambiguity	5. Business Acumen
25. Hiring and Staffing	19. Developing Direct	12. Conflict Management
46. Perspective	Reports and Others	17. Decision Quality
58. Strategic Agility	36. Motivating Others	39. Organizing
64. Understanding Others	51. Problem Solving	47. Planning
	56. Sizing Up People	

Dimension VI: Managing Profitability and Delivering Value

Cluster O: Basis for Competitive Advantage

Item15. Be the price/value leader in our marketplace.

Strong	Some	Light
5. Business Acumen	17. Decision Quality	20. Directing Others
15. Customer Focus	28. Innovation Management	33. Listening
24. Functional/Technical Skills	47. Planning	35. Managing and
51. Problem Solving	50. Priority Setting	Measuring Work
53. Drive for Results	52. Process Management	39. Organizing
63. Total Work Systems	58. Strategic Agility	61. Technical Learning
		64. Understanding Others

Cluster O: Basis for Competitive Advantage (continued)

Item 35. Be the low-cost producer or provider in our marketplace.

Strong	Some	Light
15. Customer Focus	5. Business Acumen	12. Conflict Management
16. Timely Decision Making	35. Managing and	28. Innovation Management
24. Functional/Technical Skills	Measuring Work	36. Motivating Others
50. Priority Setting	37. Negotiating	47. Planning
52. Process Management	39. Organizing	
53. Drive for Results	51. Problem Solving	
63. Total Work Systems	61. Technical Learning	

Item 55. Be the premium/quality niche provider.

Strong	Some	Light
15. Customer Focus	33. Listening	5. Business Acumen
17. Decision Quality	51. Problem Solving	46. Perspective
24. Functional/Technical Skills	53. Drive for Results	52. Process Management
28. Innovation Management	58. Strategic Agility	64. Understanding Others
63. Total Work Systems	65. Managing Vision and Purpose	

Item 74. Be the customer-service leader in our marketplace.

Strong	Some	Light
1. Action Oriented	12. Conflict Management	3. Approachability
5. Business Acumen	25. Hiring and Staffing	21. Managing Diversity
15. Customer Focus	36. Motivating Others	26. Humor
16. Timely Decision Making	37. Negotiating	29. Integrity and Trust
18. Delegation	50. Priority Setting	34. Managerial Courage
31. Interpersonal Savvy	51. Problem Solving	41. Patience
33. Listening	52. Process Management	48. Political Savvy
56. Sizing Up People	64. Understanding Others	53. Drive for Results
63. Total Work Systems		

Item 88. Continuously enter, create, and grow new markets.

Strong	Some	Light
1. Action Oriented	5. Business Acumen	2. Dealing with Ambiguity
15. Customer Focus	16. Timely Decision Making	14. Creativity
28. Innovation Management	32. Learning on the Fly	36. Motivating Others
46. Perspective	47. Planning	39. Organizing
50. Priority Setting	58. Strategic Agility	43. Perseverance
53. Drive for Results	61. Technical Learning	65. Managing Vision and Purpose

Cluster P: Supply Chain Management (from Raw Material to Customer)

Item 16. Use our edge in supply chain management to compete.

Strong	Some	Light
5. Business Acumen	15. Customer Focus	14. Creativity
17. Decision Quality	37. Negotiating	16. Timely Decision Making
24. Functional/Technical Skills	50. Priority Setting	51. ProblemSolving
39. Organizing	52. Process Management	59. Managing Through Systems
47. Planning	53. Drive for Results	64. Understanding Others
58. Strategic Agility	63. Total Work Systems	65. Managing Vision and Purpose

Cluster P: Supply Chain Management (continued)

Item 36. Have a set of metrics to monitor our supply chain efficiently and effectively.

Strong	Some	Light
5. Business Acumen	2. Dealing with Ambiguity	38. Organizational Agility
35. Managing and	50. Priority Setting	62. Time Management
Measuring Work	53. Drive for Results	63. Total Work Systems
39. Organizing	59. Managing Through	
47. Planning	Systems	
51. Problem Solving	61. Technical Learning	
52. Process Management		

Item 56. Have more effective supplier and vendor relationships than our competitors.

Strong	Some	Light
27. Informing	12. Conflict Management	5. Business Acumen
29. Integrity and Trust	38. Organizational Agility	15. Customer Focus
31. Interpersonal Savvy	48. Political Savvy	35. Managing and
33. Listening	52. Process Management	Measuring Work
36. Motivating Others	56. Sizing Up People	47. Planning
37. Negotiating	59. Managing Through	50. Priority Setting
39. Organizing	Systems	63. Total Work Systems
42. Peer Relationships	60. Building Effective Teams	
	65. Managing Vision	
	and Purpose	

Item 75. Seek out and make joint ventures and strategic partnerships work.

Strong	Some	Light
1. Action Oriented	2. Dealing with Ambiguity	5. Business Acumen
12. Conflict Management	33. Listening	31. InterpersonalSavvy
15. Customer Focus	38. Organizational Agility	39. Organizing
29. Integrity and Trust	43. Perseverance	41. Patience
36. Motivating Others	48. Political Savvy	46. Perspective
37. Negotiating	58. Strategic Agility	59. Managing Through
42. Peer Relationships	60. Building Effective Teams	Systems
51. Problem Solving	65. Managing Vision	
52. Process Management	and Purpose	

Cluster Q: Running a Profitable Business

Item17. Improve profitability and business results every year.

Strong	Some	Light
5. Business Acumen	19. Developing Direct	13. Confronting Direct
15. Customer Focus	Reports and Others	Reports
17. Decision Quality	28. Innovation Management	16. Timely Decision Making
25. Hiring and Staffing	50. Priority Setting	39. Organizing
35. Managing and	51. Problem Solving	47. Planning
Measuring Work	52. Process Management	58. Strategic Agility
53. Drive for Results	63. Total Work Systems	61. Technical Learning

Cluster Q: Running a Profitable Business (continued)

Item 37. Have high productivity; use resources efficiently.

Strong	Some	Light
35. Managing and Measuring Work	16. Timely Decision Making	5. Business Acumen
	20. Directing Others	27. Informing
39. Organizing	36. Motivating Others	32. Learning on the Fly
50. Priority Setting	47. Planning	43. Perseverance
52. Process Management	51. Problem Solving	60. Building Effective Teams
61. Technical Learning	53. Drive for Results	62. Time Management
63. Total Work Systems		

Item 57. Have predictable financial results.

Strong	Some	Light
5. Business Acumen	39. Organizing	16. Timely Decision Making
15. Customer Focus	51. Problem Solving	36. Motivating Others
35. Managing and Measuring Work	52. Process Management	59. Managing Through Systems
47. Planning	58. Strategic Agility	65. Managing Vision and Purpose
50. Priority Setting	63. Total Work Systems	
53. Drive for Results		

Cluster R: Creating and Sustaining Value

Item18: Deliver value to our investors and other relevant shareholders.

Strong	Some	Light
5. Business Acumen	17. Decision Quality	9. Command Skills
15. Customer Focus	28. Innovation Management	16. Timely Decision Making
50. Priority Setting	32. Learning on the Fly	46. Perspective
51. Problem Solving	39. Organizing	47. Planning
53. Drive for Results	43. Perseverance	65. Managing Vision and Purpose
58. Strategic Agility	52. Process Management	

Item 38. Deliver value to our customers.

Strong	Some	Light
15. Customer Focus	5. Business Acumen	9. Command Skills
16. Timely Decision Making	28. Innovation Management	12. Conflict Management
33. Listening	39. Organizing	36. Motivating Others
51. Problem Solving	50. Priority Setting	37. Negotiating
53. Drive for Results	63. Total Work Systems	40. Dealing with Paradox
58. Strategic Agility	64. Understanding Others	46. Perspective
	65. Managing Vision and Purpose	52. Process Management

THE 67 LEADERSHIP ARCHITECT® COMPETENCIES

1. Action Oriented
2. *Dealing with** Ambiguity
3. Approachability
4. Boss Relationships
5. Business Acumen
6. Career Ambition
7. Caring About Direct Reports
8. Comfort Around Higher Management
9. Command Skills
10. Compassion
11. Composure
12. Conflict Management
13. Confronting Direct Reports
14. Creativity
15. Customer Focus
16. *Timely* Decision Making
17. Decision Quality
18. Delegation
19. Developing Direct Reports and Others
20. Directing Others
21. *Managing* Diversity
22. Ethics and Values
23. Fairness to Direct Reports
24. Functional/Technical Skills
25. Hiring and Staffing
26. Humor
27. Informing
28. Innovation Management
29. Integrity and Trust
30. Intellectual Horsepower
31. Interpersonal Savvy
32. Learning on the Fly
33. Listening
34. Managerial Courage
35. Managing and Measuring Work
36. Motivating Others
37. Negotiating
38. Organizational Agility
39. Organizing
40. *Dealing with* Paradox
41. Patience
42. Peer Relationships
43. Perseverance
44. Personal Disclosure
45. Personal Learning
46. Perspective
47. Planning
48. Political Savvy
49. Presentation Skills
50. Priority Setting
51. Problem Solving
52. Process Management
53. *Drive for* Results
54. Self-Development
55. Self-Knowledge
56. Sizing Up People
57. Standing Alone
58. Strategic Agility
59. *Managing Through* Systems
60. *Building Effective* Teams
61. Technical Learning
62. Time Management
63. Total Work Systems
64. Understanding Others
65. *Managing* Vision and Purpose
66. Work/Life Balance
67. Written Communications

* Note: Italicized words are not alphabetized.

Cluster S: Filling the Talent Bench (continued)

Item 59. Accurately differentiate our people based on potential (high, moderate, low).

Strong	Some	Light
2. Dealing with Ambiguity	52. Process Management	17. Decision Quality
9. Command Skills	57. Standing Alone	33. Listening
12. Conflict Management	58. Strategic Agility	
13. Confronting Direct Reports		
34. Managerial Courage		
46. Perspective		
56. Sizing Up People		

Item 77. Accurately distinguish between our top, middle, and bottom performers.

Strong	Some	Light
12. Conflict Management	9. Command Skills	2. Dealing with Ambiguity
13. Confronting Direct Reports	17. Decision Quality	37. Negotiating
35. Managing and Measuring Work	33. Listening	
53. Drive for Results	57. Standing Alone	
56. Sizing Up People		

Item 89. Have senior management and/or the board actively engaged in our talent management process.

Strong	Some	Light
12. Conflict Management	8. Comfort Around Higher Management	7. Caring About Direct Reports
36. Motivating Others	9. Command Skills	21. Managing Diversity
47. Planning	33. Listening	34. Managerial Courage
52. Process Management	58. Strategic Agility	41. Patience
62. Time Management	65. Managing Vision and Purpose	46. Perspective

Item 94. Use job assignments to build new skills in high-potential employees.

Strong	Some	Light
2. Dealing with Ambiguity	16. Timely Decision Making	12. Conflict Management
18. Delegation	37. Negotiating	17. Decision Quality
19. Developing Direct Reports and Others	40. Dealing with Paradox	38. Organizational Agility
36. Motivating Others	51. Problem Solving	46. Perspective
47. Planning	57. Standing Alone	50. Priority Setting
56. Sizing Up People		52. Process Management
58. Strategic Agility		

Cluster R: Creating and Sustaining Value (continued)

Item 58. Deliver value (workplace, job, career) to our employees.

Strong	Some	Light
18. Delegation	7. Caring About	10. Compassion
19. Developing Direct	Direct Reports	12. Conflict Management
Reports and Others	23. Fairness to Direct Reports	13. Confronting Direct Reports
20. Directing Others	25. Hiring and Staffing	21. Managing Diversity
33. Listening	27. Informing	22. Ethics and Values
35. Managing and	29. Integrity and Trust	26. Humor
Measuring Work	31. Interpersonal Savvy	34. Managerial Courage
36. Motivating Others	53. Drive for Results	65. Managing Vision
56. Sizing Up People	66. Work / Life Balance	and Purpose
60. Building Effective Teams		

Item 76. Deliver value to the communities in which we operate.

Strong	Some	Light
15. Customer Focus	12. Conflict Management	10. Compassion
21. Managing Diversity	22. Ethics and Values	51. Problem Solving
33. Listening	31. Interpersonal Savvy	62. Time Management
40. Dealing with Paradox	64. Understanding Others	
46. Perspective		
48. Political Savvy		

Dimension VII: Developing Future Leaders

Cluster S: Filling the Talent Bench

Item19. Have a well-supported process in place to identify and develop the next generation of leaders.

Strong	Some	Light
2. Dealing with Ambiguity	12. Conflict Management	18. Delegation
13. Confronting Direct	17. DecisionQuality	33. Listening
Reports	21. Managing Diversity	47. Planning
19. Developing Direct	25. Hiring and Staffing	62. Time Management
Reports and Others	46. Perspective	
52. Process Management		
56. Sizing Up People		
58. Strategic Agility		

Item 39. Move people across functional, geographic, and business unit boundaries for development as future leaders.

Strong	Some	Light
19. Developing Direct	2. Dealing with Ambiguity	12. Conflict Management
Reports and Others	36. Motivating Others	21. Managing Diversity
38. Organizational Agility	40. Dealing with Paradox	25. Hiring and Staffing
46. Perspective	42. Peer Relationships	37. Negotiating
47. Planning	51. Problem Solving	
56. Sizing Up People	52. Process Management	
58. Strategic Agility		

Cluster S: Filling the Talent Bench (continued)

Item 95. Acquire talent from outside as needed for key positions.

Strong	Some	Light
12. Conflict Management	5. Business Acumen	2. Dealing with Ambiguity
13. Confronting Direct	21. Managing Diversity	9. Command Skills
Reports	32. Learning on the Fly	34. Managerial Courage
16. Timely Decision Making	33. Listening	37. Negotiating
17. Decision Quality	36. Motivating Others	50. Priority Setting
25. Hiring and Staffing	58. Strategic Agility	57. Standing Alone
46. Perspective		
56. Sizing Up People		

Dimension VIII: Governance

Cluster T: Managing in the Best Way

Item 20. Select and shape a board of directors that adds value.

Strong	Some	Light
12. Conflict Management	5. Business Acumen	18. Delegation
25. Hiring and Staffing	8. Comfort Around	19. Developing Direct
27. Informing	Higher Management	Reports and Others
36. Motivating Others	9. Command Skills	34. Managerial Courage
47. Planning	17. Decision Quality	37. Negotiating
56. Sizing Up People	21. Managing Diversity	48. Political Savvy
58. Strategic Agility	46. Perspective	65. Managing Vision and Purpose
	52. Process Management	

Item 40. Actively engage the board of directors in the business.

Strong	Some	Light
8. Comfort Around	5. Business Acumen	31. Interpersonal Savvy
Higher Management	12. Conflict Management	37. Negotiating
18. Delegation	39. Organizing	49. Presentation Skills
27. Informing	48. Political Savvy	60. Building Effective Teams
33. Listening	52. Process Management	65. Managing Vision
36. Motivating Others	58. Strategic Agility	and Purpose
46. Perspective		

Item 60. Effectively utilize outside resources (auditors, consultants, advisors, experts).

Strong	Some	Light
12. Conflict Management	2. Dealing with Ambiguity	5. Business Acumen
18. Delegation	39. Organizing	28. Innovation Management
25. Hiring and Staffing	47. Planning	34. Managerial Courage
33. Listening	52. Process Management	37. Negotiating
46. Perspective	53. Drive for Results	40. Dealing with Paradox
50. Priority Setting	56. Sizing Up People	59. Managing Through Systems
51. Problem Solving	60. Building Effective Teams	64. Understanding Others

Cluster T: Managing in the Best Way (continued)

Item 78. Manage the enterprise with appropriate transparency and openness.

Strong	Some	Light
23. Fairness to Direct Reports	8. Comfort Around Higher Management	3. Approachability
27. Informing	12. Conflict Management	11. Composure
29. Integrity and Trust	13. Confronting Direct Reports	33. Listening
44. Personal Disclosure	22. Ethics and Values	40. Dealing with Paradox
57. Standing Alone	34. Managerial Courage	45. Personal Learning